THE MENTAL HEALTH ACT COMMISSION

SEVENTH BIENNIAL REPORT

1995–97

Laid before Parliament by the Secretary of State for Health pursuant to Section 121(10) of the Mental Health Act 1983.

London: The Stationery Office

Applications for reproduction should be made in writing to The Copyright Unit, Her Majesty's Stationery Office, St. Clements House, 2–16 Colegate, Norwich NR3 1BQ

ISBN 0 11 321874 5

Printed in the UK for The Stationery Office
0 11 321874 5/1 07/97 C30 10170

CONTENTS

CHAIRMAN'S FOREWORD

The period since the last Biennial Report has seen the implementation of the substantial changes to the Mental Health Act Commission's structure and operation which that Report described. These changes have, as intended, enabled the Commission to make more visits to hospitals and private mental nursing homes, to see more detained patients, to target some of its activities to issues of particular concern, and to make better use of the information which it collects to monitor its own performance along with the performance of others.

The Commission's strengthened visiting capacity is no less than necessary in view of the 43% increase in the number of Mental Health Act admissions between 1990 and 1996 together with the substantial growth in the number of units which care for detained patients. This increased level of activity has been achieved not only without any increase in the Commission's resources, but is currently being maintained in the face of a 3% cut. This will not be sustainable for long and, without some increase in its funding, the Commission's capacity to perform its basic statutory duties will be seriously compromised.

This Report represents the distillation of the Commission's corporate experience of 1222 visits to hospitals and private mental nursing homes between 1 July l995 and 31 March 1997. The themes which recur throughout the Report represent important current features of services for detained patients as well as some major concerns of the Commission. In its last two Reports, the over-riding concern was bed pressure. Many, but not all, acute services are still under intense pressure, especially in London, as they cope with an increased proportion of detained patients and also with an increase in the amount and degree of disturbed behaviour. Allied with this and of growing concern to the Commission is the variation between units in the standard of the care which detained patients are receiving. Members of the Commission are seeing too many wards where staff interaction with patients is minimal, where very little structured activity takes place, where treatment plans and the Care Programme Approach are more a matter of form than substance and where too many patients face endless barren days with the administration of medicine as the main therapeutic component of their day. We know that pressures on beds and staff time, shortages of psychiatrists, psychologists and occupational therapists all contribute to this situation but they do not fully explain or justify it. The focus of public and political attention over the past few years has been on community care. We now need to ensure that the large increase in the use of the Mental Health Act is accompanied by a commensurate interest in the standards of service given to those with serious mental illness while they are in hospital and that good quality care for detained patients is more consistently achieved.

The position of detained women patients is a similar concern on all too many Commission Visits. As the Commission's National Visit confirmed, the majority of these patients still lack truly private sleeping, washing and toilet facilities. It is an unacceptable irony that many women patients, detained in the interests of their health or their safety, find themselves in hospital conditions that not only feel threatening but, in fact, offer inadequate safety and privacy. The recent welcome direction to Health Authorities has emphasized the needs of mentally ill patients for accomodation which ensures privacy and dignity. The Commission's experience indicates that this will require substantial resources. Meanwhile hospitals will need to be vigilant and ingenious in their efforts to ensure the safety and privacy of detained women patients who are at a particular disadvantage in matters of choice.

The Commission's more systematic collection of data about its customers has been quick to reveal that ethnic monitoring, which has been a mandatory requirement since April 1995, is still patchy and flawed in its implementation. As this hampers the Commission in its ability to monitor the rights and interests of detained patients from black and ethnic minority communities, so it must impede the ability of providers to do the same for the care and treatment which they provide. It may be time for ethnic monitoring to be made a statutory requirement for health and social services as it is in the criminal justice system.

The Commission shares the widespread disappointment at the recent events in Ashworth and it welcomes the statutory Inquiry set up by the Secretary of State. The Commission is in the process of examining its own performance in relation to the events at the heart of the Inquiry so as to learn any lessons for its work which might also be of help to the Inquiry in formulating recommendations for the future. The events in the High Security Hospitals draw attention yet again to the urgent need to rethink the legislative and institutional response to personality disorder in the present state of knowledge about its treatability. Above all, they emphasize once more that the reform of the size and role of those hospitals which provide high secure care must not be further delayed. Meanwhile, with the understandable anxiety created by the allegations which have prompted the Inquiry, the Commission attaches particular importance to ensuring that the proper balance is maintained between institutional responsibilities and individual rights.

The publicity attending these events has raised again in a particularly acute form the tension between the legitimate and, indeed, necessary interest of the press in such matters, the distress caused to the uninvolved majority of patients in the High Security Hospitals by the nature and tenor of the reporting, and its impact on public attitudes to the generality of psychiatric patients. I am, therefore, very pleased to have the opportunity to express publicly the Commission's gratitude to the Press Complaints Commission for the interest it is taking in promoting balanced and accurate reporting of the issues surrounding mental disorder and for its initiative in bringing together the parties to this debate in the interests of better mutual understanding. There is every reason to hope that these efforts will be fruitful.

Ruth Runciman

RHAGAIR Y CADEIRYDD

Y mae'r cyfnod ers yr Adroddiad Dwyflynyddol diwethaf wedi gweld gweithredu'r newidiadau helaeth yn strwythur a gweithredu'r Comisiwn Deddf Iechyd Meddwl a ddisgrifiwyd yn yr adroddiad hwnnw. Y mae'r newidiadau hyn, fel y bwriadwyd iddynt, wedi galluogi'r Comisiwn i wneud mwy o ymweliadau ag ysbytai a chartrefi ymgeledd iechyd meddwl preifat, i weld mwy o gleifion dan orchymyn, i dargedu rhai o'i weithgareddau at faterion o bryder arbennig, ac i wneud gwell defnydd o'r wybodaeth y mae'n ei gasglu i fonitro ei berfformiad ef ei hun ynghyd â pherfformiadau gan eraill.

Nid yw'r cryfhad yng ngallu'r Comisiwn i ymweld yn ddim mwy nag sy'n angenrheidiol yng ngwyneb y cynnydd o 45% fu yn y derbyniadau Deddf Iechyd Meddwl rhwng 1990 a 1996 ynghyd â thwf sylweddol yn y nifer o unedau sy'n gofalu am gleifion dan orchymyn. Y mae'r cynnydd hwn yn lefel y gweithgarwch wedi ei gyflawni nid yn unig heb unrhyw gynnydd yn adnoddau'r Comisiwn, ond y mae ar hyn o bryd yn cael ei gynnal yng ngwyneb toriad o 3%. Ni bydd modd cynnal hyn yn hir iawn ac os na bydd rhyw gynnydd yn y nawdd ariannol, fe fydd gallu'r Comisiwn i weithredu ei ddyletswyddau statudol sylfaenol mewn perygl difrifol.

Y mae'r Adroddiad hwn yn ddistylliad o brofiad corfforaethol y Comisiwn sy'n cynnwys 1222 o ymweliadau ag ysbytai a chartrefi ymgeledd iechyd meddwl preifat rhwng Gorffennaf 1af 1995 a Mawrth 31ain 1997. Y mae'r themâu sy'n cael eu hailadrodd drwy gydol yr Adroddiad yn cynrychioli materion gwasanaeth cyfredol pwysig ar gyfer cleifion dan orchymyn yn ogystal â rhai o brif bryderon y Comisiwn. Yn y ddau Adroddiad diwethaf, y pryder mwyaf dybryd oedd y galw am welyau. Y mae llawer, ond nid pob, gwasanaeth dwys, yn parhau i fod dan bwysau mawr, yn enwedig yn Llundain, fel y maent yn ymdopi â chyfran gynyddol o gleifion dan orchymyn ac hefyd gyda chynnydd ym maint a graddfa ymddygiad cynhyrfus. Ynghlwm â hyn ac o bryder cynyddol i'r Comisiwn, y mae'r amrywiaeth mewn safonau rhwng unedau parthed cynnwys y gofal y mae'r cleifion dan orchymyn yn ei dderbyn. Y mae aelodau'r Comisiwn yn gweld gormod o wardiau ble mae cydadwaith y staff â chleifion yn fach iawn, ble nad oes ond ychydig o weithgaredd strwythuredig yn digwydd, ble mae'r cynlluniau triniaeth a'r dull gweithredu rhaglen ofal yn fwy o ffurf nag o sylwedd a ble mae gormod o gleifion yn wynebu dyddiau diffaith di ben draw gyda dosbarthu moddion yn brif gydran therapiwtig eu dydd. Fe wyddom bod y pwysau sydd ar welyau ac amser y staff, prinder seiciatryddion, a seicolegwyr a therapyddion galwedigaethol i gyd yn cyfrannu tuag at y sefyllfa hon ond nid ydynt yn ei hegluro nac yn ei chyfiawnhau yn llawn. Fe fu sylw'r cyhoeddus a'r sylw gwleidyddol yn canolbwyntio ar ofal yn y gymuned dros yr ychydig flynyddoedd diwethaf. Y mae angen i ni yn awr sicrhau bod y cynnydd mawr fu yn nefnydd y Ddeddf Iechyd Meddwl yn cael ei ddilyn gan ddiddordeb cyffelyb yn safonau'r gwasanaethau a roddir i'r rhai hynny sydd ag afiechyd meddwl difrifol tra maent hwy yn yr ysbyty a bod gofal o ansawdd uchel yn cael ei gyflawni'n fwy cyson ar gyfer cleifion dan orchymyn

Y mae safle merched o gleifion dan orchymyn hefyd yn bryder cyffelyb ar lawer gormod o ymweliadau'r Comisiwn. Fel y mae Ymweliad Cenedlaethol y Comisiwn yn cadarnhau, y mae'r rhan fwyaf o'r cleifion hyn yn parhau i fod heb gyfleusterau cysgu, ymolchi a thoiled gwirioneddol breifat. Y mae'n eironi annerbyniol bod llawer o gleifion benywaidd, dan orchymyn yn rhinwedd eu hiechyd neu eu diogelwch, yn eu cael eu hunain mewn amodau ysbyty sydd nid yn unig yn teimlo'n fygythiol ond sydd, fel mater o ffaith, yn cynnig diogelwch a phreifatrwydd annigonol. Y mae'r gorchymyn diweddar, sydd yn destun croeso i Awdurdodau Iechyd wedi pwysleisio anghenion cleifion sâl eu meddwl am lety sy'n sicrhau preifatrwydd ac urddas. Y mae profiad y Comisiwn yn dynodi y bydd hyn yn gofyn am adnoddau sylweddol ac, yn y cyfamser, fe fydd angen i ysbytai fod ar eu gwyliadwriaeth ac yn ddyfeisgar yn eu hymdrechion i wneud yn siwr o ddiogelwch a phreifatrwydd cleifion benywaidd dan orchymyn sydd o dan anfantais neilltuol o safbwynt dewis.

Mewn byr dro fe fu i gasgliad mwy systematig y Comisiwn ar ddata ynglyn â chwsmeriaid ddangos bod monitro ethnig, a fu yn ofyniad gorfodol ers Ebrill 1995, yn ysbeidiol ac yn ddiffygiol yn y modd y'i gweithredir. Gan fod hyn yn rhwystr i'r Comisiwn er ei alluogi i fonitro hawliau a buddiannau cleifion dan orchymyn o gymunedau duon a lleiafrifoedd ethnig, y mae'n rhaid felly ei fod yn llesteirio gallu'r darparwyr i wneud yr un peth ar gyfer y gofal a'r driniaeth y maent yn eu darparu. Efallai ei bod hi'n bryd gwneud monitro ethnig yn ofyniad statudol ar gyfer iechyd a gwasanaethau cymdeithasol fel y mae yn y system cyfiawnder troseddol.

Y mae'r Comisiwn yn rhannu'r siom cyffredinol oherwydd yr hyn a ddigwyddodd yn ddiweddar yn Ashworth ac y mae'n croesawu'r archwiliad statudol a roddwyd ar waith gan yr Ysgrifennydd Gwladol. Y mae'r Comisiwn wrthi ar hyn o bryd yn archwilio ei berfformiad ef ei hun parthed y digwyddiadau sy'n ganolog i'r archwiliad er mwyn dysgu gwersi ar gyfer ei waith a all fod o gymorth i'r archwiliad wrth lunio argymhellion ar gyfer y dyfodol. Y mae'r digwyddiadau fu yn yr Ysbytai Diogelwch Uchel yn tynnu sylw unwaith eto am yr angen i brysuro i ailfeddwl am yr ymatebiadau cyfreithiol a sefydliadol i anhwylder personoliaeth o ystyried stad bresennol yr wybodaeth am driniaethau. Yn anad dim, y maent yn pwysleisio unwaith eto na ellir gohirio ymhellach ar ddiwygio maint a swyddogaeth yr ysbytai sy'n darparu gofal diogelwch uchel. Yn y cyfamser, gyda'r pryderon dealladwy a godir gan y cyhuddiadau sydd wedi sbarduno'r archwiliad, y mae'r Comisiwn yn rhoi pwysigrwydd neilltuol ar sicrhau bod y cyfartaledd priodol yn cael ei gynnal rhwng cyfrifoldebau sefydliadol a hawliau unigol.

Y mae'r cyhoeddusrwydd sy'n dilyn y digwyddiadau hyn wedi codi mewn modd neilltuol o ddifrifol y tensiwn sydd rhwng yr hyn sy'n ddiddordeb cyfreithlon ac, yn wir, yn ddiddordeb angenrheidiol gan y wasg mewn materion o'r fath, y mae'r gofid a achosir i'r mwyafrif o'r cleifion yn yr Ysbytai Diogelwch Uchel nad ydynt yn rhan o'r achos gan natur a tÿn y gohebu, a'i effaith ar ymagweddu cyhoeddus ar gleifion seiceiatrig yn gyffredinol. Yr wyf, gan hynny, yn falch iawn o gael y cyfle i ddatgan yn gyhoeddus ddiolchgarwch y Comisiwn i Gomisiwn Cwynion y Wasg am y diddordeb y mae yn ei ddangos mewn hyrwyddo gohebu cytbwys a chywir ar faterion sy'n cwmpasu anhwylder meddyddiol ac am ei flaengaredd mewn dwyn at ei gilydd y partÿon yn y ddadl hon er lles gwell cyd-ddealltwriaeth. Y mae pob rheswm dros obeithio y bydd yr ymdrechion hyn yn gynhyrchiol.

Ruth Runciman

Chapter 1

The Commission's Function and Organisation

Summary

The Biennial Report covers the period 1st July 1995 to 31st March 1997.

During this period, key changes have been implemented in the organisation of the Commission, the objectives of which are to increase the quality and quantity of contact between Commission members and detained patients and to make more effective use of the information collected from visits and other activities.

Besides its routine activity of visiting hospitals and mental nursing homes, investigating complaints that fall within its statutory remit and administering the consent to treatment safeguards in the Act, the Commission has:

- *submitted detailed recommendations to the Secretary of State for Health for the revision of the Mental Health Act Code of Practice;*

- *introduced a Reporting Procedure for Issues of Special Concern;*

- *issued five Guidance Notes (formerly called Practice Notes) and one Position Paper, generally referring to matters not included in the Code of Practice;*

- *issued five leaflets providing information for detained patients;*

- *strengthened its policies on Equal Opportunities;*

- *undertaken a National Visit, which enabled the Commission to obtain a nation-wide picture of important aspects of the care of detained patients.*

1 The Commission's Function

1.1 Statutory Responsibilities

The duties of the Mental Health Act Commission have been described in previous Reports. Established in 1983 as a Special Health Authority, its essential role is to keep under review the implementation of the 1983 Mental Health Act as it relates to patients detained under its provisions. It does this by visiting hospitals and mental nursing homes, interviewing detained patients in private and producing reports of its findings. It also investigates complaints that fall within its statutory remit, for example, where a detained patient is dissatisfied with the response to a complaint they have made to the managers of the hospital where they are detained.

The Commission administers the consent to treatment safeguards in the Act, principally by the appointment of suitably qualified doctors - 'Second Opinion Appointed Doctors' (SOADs) - who have to certify that certain treatments are appropriate before they can be given in the absence of the detained patient's consent.

The Commission monitors the implementation of the Mental Health Act Code of Practice, issued by the Department of Health and the Welsh Office, providing guidance on the admission of detained patients and their care and treatment. It submits periodically to the Secretaries of State suggestions for changes in subsequent editions of the Code. It is empowered to review the decisions of High Security Hospital Managers to withhold patients' incoming or outgoing post. The Commission also offers advice to Ministers on matters falling within its remit.

The Commission is required to publish a Biennial Report on its work. **This is the seventh such Report covering the period 1st July 1995 to 31st March 1997.** The slightly shorter period than the usual two years is a one-off adjustment to align the Commission's financial and reporting cycle.

1.2 Re-organisation of the Commission

The restructuring of the Commission, described in the last Biennial Report, was completed by 1st November 1995. The Commission now comprises 191 members, including 95 visiting members, all appointed by the Secretary of State for Health or

Secretary of State for Wales. The restructuring of the Commission was accompanied by the introduction of a more open process of recruitment by public advertisement and interview prior to recommendations about appointments being made to the Secretaries of State. All newly-appointed members receive induction training. In 1996 the Commission introduced an informal performance review procedure for its members.

With the exception of the Chairman, Vice-Chairman and four Commissioners who undertake specialist tasks, every Commission member is attached to either one of the Commission's seven regionally-based Commission Visiting Teams (CVTs) or to one of the three High Security Hospital Panels. The areas covered by each CVT are shown in the map below:

Figure 1: Map showing Commission areas in England and Wales

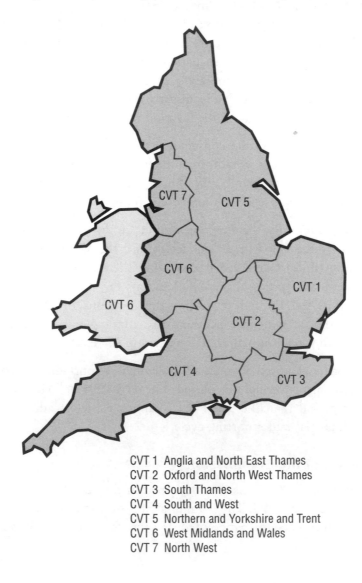

CVT 1 Anglia and North East Thames
CVT 2 Oxford and North West Thames
CVT 3 South Thames
CVT 4 South and West
CVT 5 Northern and Yorkshire and Trent
CVT 6 West Midlands and Wales
CVT 7 North West

The Teams and Panels have around 18 members (save for CVT5 which has rather more and covers the largest of the 7 areas), each including a range of disciplines. For each Team or Panel, a Convenor is appointed who has overall responsibility for the work, organising the rota of Visits and allocating members to Visits according to the numbers of patients involved and the tasks to be undertaken. Each Team and Panel has the support of nominated officers at Commission Headquarters.

Commission members take turns to lead the small groups who undertake the Visits to hospitals and take responsibility for writing the Visit Reports. Visiting members are primarily, but not exclusively, involved in the interviewing of detained patients. In order that Commission members on Panels visiting the High Security Hospitals should also have working knowledge of the services provided by the Regional Secure Units (RSUs), they are being included with the CVT members when Visits to RSUs are undertaken in 1997/8.

New arrangements, including differentiating the duties of Commission members and Commission visiting members, were started in November 1995. Greater specialisation amongst the members of the Commission was introduced, with varying remuneration rates to reflect differing responsibilities.

Two Commission members are based in the Nottingham office: the Policy Co-ordinator, whose task is to lead the Commission's development of policy and the Complaints Co-ordinator who leads the Commission's specialist Complaints Team.

Commission members and visiting members are drawn from medicine, nursing, psychology, social work, the law and various other relevant specialities, as well as those with a lay interest in mental health issues. On average, they commit two to three days a month to Commission activity. Just under half are women. A list of all those who have been members of the Commission in the period under review can be found at Appendix 1.

The Commission appoints registered medical practitioners and others to undertake the duties set out in Part IV of the Mental Health Act. These are described further in Chapter 5. A list of Second Opinion Appointed Doctors and the Panel of Appointed Persons (for Section 57) can be found at Appendix 2.

On 1st November 1995, overall responsibility for the management of the Commission passed to the Commission Management Board whose members are the Commission Chairman, Vice-Chairman, three Commission members, the Chief Executive and the Director of Finance. Reporting to the Board are three principal bodies:

i the Convenors, who meet as a Group and undertake co-ordination and quality control of the Commission's visiting activities;

ii   the Policy Advisory Group, whose task is to advise the Management Board on policy issues;

iii   the Executive Management Group, made up of specialist Commission members based in Nottingham and the Executive Directors of the Commission.

In addition, there are four Special Interest Groups: Consent to Treatment, Legal and Ethical, Code of Practice and Quality Standards. Their responsibility is to advise the Commission Management Board, through the Policy Advisory Group, on issues within their remit.

1.3   The Revised Code of Practice

The current Code has been in force since November 1993 and the Commission has had the task of monitoring its implementation and submitting proposals to Ministers for changes it considers necessary or appropriate. In accordance with its obligations under Section 118 of the Act, the Department of Health issued the proposed revisions for consultation and set a deadline date for receipt of comments of February 28th 1997. Circumstances permitting, the intention is to lay the Code before Parliament for implementation a few months later in 1997. An updated edition of the Memorandum to the Mental Health Act will be published at the same time as the Code.

Because users of the Code will have become familiar with its layout, the Commission has suggested that changes to its structure and to chapter numbering be kept to a minimum. The revisions take into account the implications of recent decisions by the courts. This has been of particular importance with regard to Chapter 5, on the choice between using Section 2 or 3 for admission to hospital, and Chapter 16, about medical treatment and Second Opinions.

Some of the more significant suggested revisions include changes in:

- Chapter 2, so as to bring together the advice on communications between professionals;

- Chapter 8, on the use of Section 5(2), in the reference to lack of capacity in the definition of an informal patient;

- Chapter 13, on Guardianship, with the intention of reflecting responses to an increasing use of this provision, especially for patients with a degree of mental incapacity;

- Chapters 22 and 23, on the role of Hospital Managers and the exercise of their powers of discharge;

- Chapter 30, which covers children and young people, including an extensive revision to provide guidance for practitioners on choosing between the Mental Health Act and the Children Act for purposes of detention in hospital.

It is also proposed to include, as an appendix to the Code, details of the Practice and Guidance Notes issued periodically by the Commission (see 1.6).

1.4 Commission Finances

The Commission, as a Special Health Authority, is financed from the Health Services Parliamentary Vote by the Department of Health, with a contribution from the Welsh Office.

With the establishment of the Commission Management Board, new Standing Financial Instructions were adopted and the Board appointed a Finance Sub-Committee to assist it in the discharge of its financial responsibilities, including meeting the requirements of the Code of Conduct and Accountability for NHS Boards. The Commission's accounts are audited by the Audit Commission and from 1996 prepared on the accrual basis: i.e. recording income and expenditure when they are incurred, regardless of when the payment is received or made.

A summary of the Commission's finances can be found at Appendix 3.

1.5 Reporting Procedure For Issues Of Special Concern

The last Biennial Report registered the Commission's anxiety about a very small number of matters of serious and persistent concern that fall within its statutory remit, but remain unremedied, despite the Commission having drawn the attention of those responsible to the deficiencies. The Commission was concerned about its lack of effective sanctions, an issue that has been commented upon elsewhere (Barnes, 1996).

In 1996, Ministers endorsed a new Reporting Procedure for Issues of Special Concern. Details of the Procedure were circulated to the NHS and independent sectors, in England, prior to its implementation on 1st October 1996. The key features of the procedure are set out below.

- The Procedure will be invoked only on the authority of the Chairman. It is anticipated that the Procedure will be used rarely, since it is the Commission's experience that a high proportion of its recommendations are accepted and action taken.

- Issues appropriate for the procedure include:

    i   persistent serious breaches of the Mental Health Act and associated regulations;

THE MENTAL HEALTH ACT COMMISSION *Seventh Biennial Report*

ii   matters of persistent serious concern about the care of detained patients which are not based in statute but are of major concern and within the remit of the Commission in its monitoring of the Code of Practice.

- To invoke the procedure the Chairman writes to the provider unit or other party setting out the matter of concern and requesting a response within 14 days. What further action is taken depends on the response. Should matters continue unresolved a report is sent to the Secretary of State with copies to interested bodies. After this, further action, in consultation with the Secretary of State, may include reporting the matter in the Biennial Report, informing the press or referring the matter to the Health Service Commissioner or other relevant authorities.

1.6 Commission Publications

The Commission continues to publish Guidance Notes (formerly called Practice Notes), which give advice on matters not included in the Code of Practice. The Commission will, from time to time, also publish Position Papers, containing its views on particular issues drawn to its attention. During the reporting period five Guidance Notes have been produced, three of which draw out Mental Health Act issues of particular relevance for Registered Mental Nursing Homes, Health Authorities and GPs and two which deal with Sections 17 and 18 of the Act and anorexia nervosa. A Position Paper was issued on research involving detained patients. The full list of these publications can be found in Appendix 4.

The Commission also published five leaflets in April, 1996, giving information to detained patients about specific aspects of the Commission's role and the Act (see 3.1.3).

1.7 Equal Opportunities

The Commission is committed to the eradication of discrimination and the promotion of equal opportunities in all its services and will discharge all its duties recognising that every individual has a legal and moral right to equal and non-discriminatory high quality service. The Commission's Equal Opportunities Policy statement is at Appendix 5.

1.8 The National Visit

On November 21st 1996, the Commission conducted an unannounced National Visit, which was an unique initiative in its history. It deployed most of the members and staff of the Commission in visiting, on one day, 309 acute psychiatric admission and intensive care wards in 118 NHS Trusts across England and Wales. It enabled the

20

Commission to obtain a nation-wide picture of specific aspects of mental health provision of central importance to the care and treatment of detained patients. These were:

- the number, skill mix and deployment of staff;

- the adequacy and understanding of policy and procedures about leave for detained patients;

- the privacy and safety of women patients.

The Visit was undertaken in collaboration with The Sainsbury Centre for Mental Health, who analysed and reported the findings (The Mental Health Act Commission, 1997). The findings present a snapshot view of acute inpatient facilities which, because of the robust methodology employed, provide a representative picture of these facilities across England and Wales. Reference is made to these findings in the relevant sections of this Report.

1.9 Examples of Good and Bad Practice

Examples used to illustrate practice points appear in many of the chapters in this Biennial Report. Most are taken from Visit Reports and it is Commission policy to name the Trusts to which they refer. They are chosen to illustrate good or bad practice and the comments made often apply equally to many other providers. Where particular events or circumstances are cited, it must not be taken to necessarily imply that they are typical of the overall practices of the Trust in question.

Visit Reports commend good practice as well as criticising bad. If the examples in this Report seem to relate more often to bad practice that is because they have been selected to point up matters causing concern. However, the Commission is fully appreciative of the continuing improvements in many aspects of the care of detained patients.

Chapter 2

Commission Visits

Summary

The Commission has developed more detailed guidance on the purpose and conduct of Visits to mental health units and Social Services Departments and is operating a revised schedule for Visits. Full Visits occur less frequently, but other Visits, targeting specific concerns or focusing on interviewing patients occur more often. Every patient interviewed by a Commission member now receives a letter summarising the main points discussed and any action proposed.

There have been substantial changes in the structure of mental health services, resulting in a greater number and diversity of units able to admit detained patients and this has had an impact on the Commission's programme of Visits. The substantial numbers of patients interviewed has provided the Commission with a fair sampling of detained patients and of the issues that concern them. The Commission has achieved its target of contacting, each year, all detained patients in the High Security Hospitals and interviewing those who wish to be seen.

The most frequent issues of concern raised by patients when they meet with Commission members are about detention, medical care services and treatment and Mental Health Review Tribunal matters.

2 Commission Visits

2.1 Visiting Organisation and Policy

2.1.1 Scope of the Visiting Remit

A large part of the work of the Commission consists of Visits by Commission members to units where there are detained patients in order to interview as many of them as wish to be seen and to observe compliance with the Act and the Department of Health's Code of Practice. The Commission's remit for this task, carried out on behalf of the Secretary of State, is set out in Section 120 of the Act as follows:

- to keep under review the exercise of the powers and duties contained in the Act which relate to detained patients and to patients liable to be detained;

- to visit and interview in private patients detained under the Act in hospitals and nursing homes.

Besides visiting hospitals and nursing homes, meetings are regularly held with representatives of Social Services Departments and the relevant health purchasing authorities.

Members are guided by the Commission's Visiting Policy and Procedures, from which the following extract is taken.

PURPOSE OF VISITS

a. Hospitals and Mental Nursing Homes

Visits by members of the Commission to hospitals and mental nursing homes have, broadly speaking, a fourfold purpose:-

i. to meet with detained patients in private, particularly those who have asked to meet members of the Commission. Meetings may be with individual patients or with groups of patients, including Patients' Councils;

ii. to observe the conditions in which patients are detained;

iii. to see how the provisions of the Mental Health Act 1983 and the Code of Practice are being applied;

iv.   to offer advice and guidance on the implementation of the Act. The highest priority should be given to meeting detained patients and to checking the detention documents.

b.   **Social Services Departments;**

The purpose of meeting representatives of Social Services Departments is to encourage a co-ordinated approach to the operation of the Act and, in particular, to keep under review:-

i.   the Social Services Departments' responses to the Act and the Code of Practice;

ii.   the process of assessment, compulsory admission and detention under the Act, including the availability of ASWs, communication with GPs, hospitals, Section 12 doctors and the emergency services;

iii.   the planning and delivery of appropriate residential places, alternatives to detention and aftercare procedures and facilities;

iv.   the extent to which hospital and community services are able to integrate all aspects of a patient's detention from the initial assessment to the termination of aftercare.

c.   **Purchasers**

The purpose of meeting representatives of the relevant purchasing authorities is to ensure that the contractual arrangements meet the needs of the detained patients, that the services being delivered meet the contractual requirements, and to help and encourage the purchasers to engage in the routine monitoring of service delivery. Meetings with both purchasers and providers should enable the Commission to gain a better insight into the quality and pattern of mental health services.

2.1.2   Revised Visiting Format

Each hospital / mental nursing home now receives a **Full Visit** at least once every two years, rather than the previous practice of an annual visit. Commission members also meet with Social Services Departments at least once every two years. Full Visits terminate with a formal meeting at which hospital staff and representatives from relevant outside agencies are normally present. In addition, there is a programme of **Patient Focused Visits,** where the emphasis is on meeting detained patients rather than reviewing the full range of services and facilities provided by the Trust. Each hospital / mental nursing home will receive at least three Patient Focused Visits in a two year period and Regional / Medium Secure Units at least one a year.

As part of the Patient Focused Visit, Commission members collect information in a standardised format on *"Matters Requiring Particular Attention"*. This enables the Commission to acquire information systematically across England and Wales on a small number of specific concerns. The procedure was introduced in 1997 and served to identify matters requiring examination on all Patient Focused Visits during the subsequent year, namely:

- Forms 38 (Certificate of Consent to Treatment)

- seclusion

- the physical examination of patients

- women's care

- ethnic monitoring

In addition, **Targeted Visits** are undertaken from time to time to examine specific issues, which may be a matter of concern in a particular unit or locality, such as the authorization and recording of Section 17 leave, bed pressures and aftercare arrangements under Section 117.

Targeted or Patient Focused Visits may sometimes be **Unannounced** or at **Short Notice**, which allows the Commission to investigate matters while normal routines are in progress.

The three High Security Hospitals are visited more frequently than other hospitals, with a greater number of unannounced Visits, which may take place during the evenings and weekends. High Security Hospital patients are generally long-stay patients and the aim is to have a meeting, or at least some meaningful contact, with every patient who wishes it, not less than once a year. Meetings take place with the Patients' Council of each High Security Hospital twice a year. The Visiting Panel members periodically examine particular issues, such as seclusion, treatment plans, access to fresh air, and provide reports to the Hospital managers. Written reports are also given to each Clinical Director on matters within their particular areas of responsibility.

All patients who have been interviewed by a member of the Commission now receive a personal letter summarising the issues raised and outlining any further action which, with the agreement of the patients, is to be taken by themselves or by the Commission. If the patient agrees, a copy of the letter may be given to the ward manager.

Reports sent to hospitals and Social Services follow a specified format, highlighting examples of good practice observed and also identifying issues which require attention and any items where specific responses are requested. Wherever appropriate, a timed programme of remedial action is requested.

The Commission does not have specific legal powers to direct that services should implement its recommendations, but in most cases its recommendations are accepted. Copies of its Reports are sent to the relevant Health Purchasers, who may make use of them when monitoring compliance with the Act and Code of Practice. The Commission has issued a Guidance Note (No. 1), *Guidance to Health Authorities: the Mental Health Act, 1983*, to help strengthen the role of Health Authorities in carrying out their responsibilities for contracting for services for detained patients.

In summary, the objectives of the new procedures are:

• to increase the quality and quantity of contact between members of the Commission and detained patients;

• to monitor more effectively the quality of the Commission's work;

• to improve the Commission's communications with detained patients;

• to make more effective use of the information and material collected during visits.

The initial data, summarised in the following section, gives some indication of how far these objectives may have been achieved in the first year of operation of the revised policy.

2.2 Analysis of Information from Visits

2.2.1 What Information is Collected

The data collection and analysis serves two purposes: to monitor the performance of the Commission itself and to observe trends in the operation of the Act. Both the quantitative and qualitative information obtained from the visiting activity of the Commission has been refined considerably since the last Biennial Report. Statistics collected include:

• the number of Commission Visits made;

• age, gender, disorder category and ethnic group of patients seen;

• issues raised by patients;

• identification and rating of issues from Visits;

• the number of Visit Reports completed within target time limits.

The Commission also collects statistics from each Trust and from mental nursing homes on the uses of selected sections of the Act and other matters concerning detained patients and is grateful to them for their co-operation. Formerly, this information was used only for pre-Visit planning purposes. The collection of this 'Hospital

Profile' data was made more systematic in 1995/96, enabling the Commission to compile and analyse information on uses of the Act during the previous financial year at local, regional and national levels. This also provides a remedy, albeit imperfect, for the gap to which the Commission has consistently drawn attention, namely the absence of any duty on hospitals to notify the Commission of all detentions and discharges, as is statutorily required in Scotland and Northern Ireland.

The Commission's Visit Reports provide in-depth information about the operation of the Mental Health Act and the quality of treatment and care of detained patients in each locality. A six-monthly summary of these reports is prepared so that instances of both good and bad practice can be followed throughout England and Wales and matters identified which need attention at local and / or national level.

2.2.2 Analysis of the Information

Mental Health Units Visited

The number of NHS hospitals and independent nursing homes able to admit detained patients and therefore requiring Commission Visits has been increasing considerably over the past few years. The increase in the proportion of beds for mental illness available in the independent sector is shown at Figure 2 (although not all the private units will be registered to take detained patients).

Figure 2: Mental illness beds – England

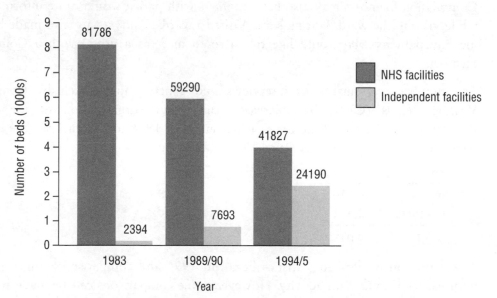

Figures taken from NHS Annual Report 1995/96. NHS Executive

The expansion of the independent sector, in particular, has major implications for the Commission visiting programme. The number of formal admissions to private nursing homes increased from 430 in 1990–91 to 790 in 1995–6 (Dept. of Health, 1997). Among the smaller nursing homes within the independent sector these patients are spread thinly, with some nursing homes having only one or two detained patients, but nevertheless requiring regular visiting. The Commission is, therefore, obliged to make an increased number of Visits, which, at April 1997, amounted to 900 in both sectors; a Visit may include more than one unit.

The Commission made a total of 1222 Visits during the 21 months of the reporting period — 474 between 1–7–95 and 31–3–96 and 748 between 1–4–96 and 31-3-97. This is slightly more (pro rata) than the previous reporting period, when 1360 Visits were made in the two years between 1993 and 1995

To achieve maximum impact the Report following a Visit needs to be prepared and dispatched to the unit concerned and to the relevant purchaser as soon as possible. A target of 5 weeks has been set, which has been achieved for 59% of reports, with a further 27% being sent within 7 weeks. The Commission recognises that there is room for improvement here.

Contact with Patients

Units are encouraged to notify patients of the date of a forthcoming Commission Visit so they can indicate in advance their wish to be seen. Apart from private *interviews*, Commission members may also have *contacts* with patients on a more informal basis, while visiting the ward. During some Visits to wards, *contacts* are also made by inviting any patients who would like to do so to meet as a group with a Commission member.

The number and quality of interviews and contacts undertaken by Commission Visiting Teams (CVTs) has increased since the reorganisation of the Visiting Procedure. During the 12 month period from April 1996 to March 1997 the numbers seen (excluding High Security Panel Visits) were:

CVT Activity 1996/7

interviews	4,714
contacts	2,301
total	7,015

The collection of detailed statistics began in 1996 and comparisons cannot be made with earlier Commission activity. However, some comparisons can be made with data on the total number of detentions in a year.

The hospital profile data for 1995/6 collected by the Commission gives the number of times the Act was used to detain patients in NHS Trusts and Mental Nursing Homes in England and Wales and is summarised in the table below.

	Number of sections	Number converted / changed	Number not converted / changed
Part 11			
Section 2	18287	2716	15571
Section 3	18032		18032
Section 4	1669	1187	482
Section 5.2	10874	6679	4195
Part 111 (S37,47,48)	1659		1659
Total	50521		39939

Explanatory note on table. The data is presented in three columns to avoid double counting where a patient has been transferred from one section to another during one hospital stay. The first column reflects total activity under the Mental Health Act. The second column gives the number of times where the section used to detain a patient has been changed. The third column shows the number of detentions; i.e. the number of times patients were made subject to at least one section of the Act during one hospital stay. The number of detentions, at 39,939, represents just over 16% of all admissions. In addition to the above, there were 1,520 applications of Section 5(4) and 1,986 reported uses of Section 136. No other data about the outcome following the use of these sections is available.

In spite of practical limits on the frequency of Visits, and the fact that many patients do not opt for an interview, it can be seen that the number of detained patients interviewed (4,714) is large enough to provide a fair sample of the range of concerns and a reasonable overview of how the Act is operating from the patients' perspective.

How far does the number of patients seen by Commissioners reflect age, gender and ethnic group of the detained patient population?

Figure 3 sets out by age and sex the patients interviewed during CVT Visits during 1996/7.

Figure 3: Patients interviewed by age and sex (CVTs)

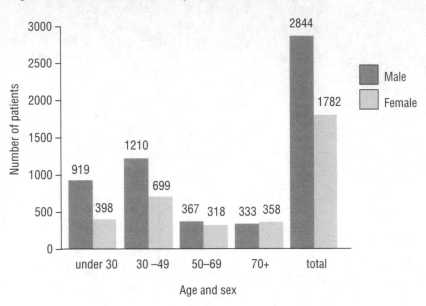

No. of meetings with age and gender assigned = 4602; no. of meetings with just gender assigned = 4626

Sixty one per cent of patients interviewed are male, although about 54% of total formal admissions to NHS facilities are male (Dept. of Health, 1997). The smaller proportion of women interviewed might be partly accounted for by the small number of elderly people, among whom women predominate, who come for interview.

Patients are not directly asked about their ethnicity when meeting with a Commission member. This information is extracted from the hospital case file, so the Commission's recording of ethnicity depends on the reliability of information collected and recorded on patients' files. The proportion 'not allocated' shows that ethnic monitoring of patients by mental health units is often incomplete.

Figure 4: CVT interviews by ethnicity (n=4714)

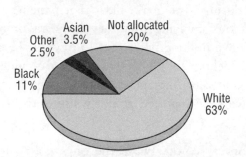

Ethnic monitoring is now a requirement (NHS Executive EL (94)77). The Commission's view on the importance of ethnic monitoring is outlined later (see 10.4.2). Ethnic monitoring has been identified as a 'matter requiring particular attention' on Visits, to enable the Commission to audit the recording of ethnicity and determine whether the ethnic coding being used corresponds to the census categories of the OPCS (Office of Population Censuses and Surveys, now The Office of National Statistics). It is recognised that sensitivity is required when recording personal data on individual patients and that it may not be possible to obtain all the necessary demographic information at the time of admission. However, records should be updated as soon as possible.

Twenty one per cent of those interviewed or contacted during Commission Visits whose ethnicity was recorded were from ethnic minority groups, but it is not known how this figure compares with the ethnicity of the total population of detained patients.

The three High Security Hospitals are visited more intensively than other hospitals. During 1996/7, there were 175 Visits undertaken. There were 1421 resident patients in these Hospitals in March 1997. The Commission has set a target that every patient has the opportunity to be seen at least once a year. This has been achieved, although not all patients wish to have an interview with a Commission member, while others may be interviewed on more than one occasion. The total activity for 1996/7 is shown in Figure 5.

Figure 5: Special hospital activity

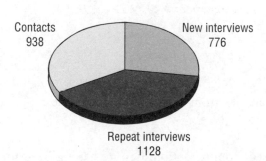

2.3   Issues Raised by Patients

Commission members during Visits make clear that patients are welcome to be interviewed in private, without implying that they have an obligation to accept. Some patients feel that they have nothing they want to discuss. There have been occasional complaints of patients feeling unduly pressured into coming for interview. On the other hand, when Commission members make informal contacts while touring a ward, patients who have been reported as not wanting to be seen sometimes ask for an interview.

Patients raise many concerns, not always the ones that come to the Commission's attention in other ways or in the order of priority that professional carers might expect. The Commission's observations on most of the issues appear later in the Report, but it is worth noting what patients themselves bring forward. Most of the issues are about the patients' own situation or treatment, but general comments for the information of the Commission are also made on matters such as hospital routines and staff attitudes. With the patients' consent (which is usually given without hesitation, because patients want staff to know their concerns), Commission members discuss issues with staff, who are nearly always sympathetic and wanting to meet patients' wishes where possible. Only a minority of unresolved personal issues lead to a formal complaint by the patient.

The topics raised during interviews with patients are now registered by marking the categories on a record form. This provides data about the most common concerns. The relative frequency of the main categories, taken from Visit Record Forms, is set out below.

Issues Raised by Patients (April — December 1996)

Loss of freedom	757	28 %
Medical care services and treatment	481	17 %
Review Tribunal matters	271	10 %
Domestic care, living arrangements	251	9 %
All other issues	952	35 %
Total issues	2712	100 %

Here are typical examples from among these categories:

Loss of Freedom

- wish to be released from detention; despite having been forewarned, many patients still express disappointment that the Commission has no power to discharge

- belief that their condition does not warrant detention

- complaints about the manner of their assessment and conveyance to hospital, especially when police have been involved

- objection to restrictions, such as confinement to ward, necessity for escorts, limited outings

- irksome rules, such as fixed bedtimes, awkward mealtimes, limited access to bed-rooms

- need to approach nurses for cigarettes, drinks, money, access to toilets

Medical Care and Treatment

- wish to reduce medication to prevent side effects

- limited opportunity to discuss treatment plan with Responsible Medical Officer

- doubts about the independence of a Second Opinion

- consent to treatment under duress

- placement in inappropriate ward or unit

- nurses too busy to talk

Tribunal Matters

- delay in securing a hearing

- RMO's report delayed

- staff reports to Tribunal unfair

- Tribunal hearing was upsetting

- delay in implementing conditional discharge

- not fully informed of rights

Domestic Care, Living Arrangements

- boredom, lack of ward activity

- diet monotonous, servings cold, vegetarian or ethnic diets inadequate

- lack of privacy

- inadequate control of other patients' noisiness, aggression, sexual impropriety or offensiveness.

Chapter 3

Admission and Detention

Summary

There has been a substantial increase in the number of formal admissions over recent years, although in 1995/6 there are signs of levelling off. The Commission would welcome further research into the factors underlying the statistical trends.

Some provider units need to enhance their procedures for informing patients of their rights.

The Commission is aware of the arguments for and against removing from Managers the power to discharge, but it is concerned that any change should not affect Managers' important role in overseeing the care of detained patients and ensuring compliance with the Act.

In view of the marked variations between units in the frequency of application of Section 5(2), the Commission would like to see audits of this Section wherever high usage occurs. Implementation of Section 5(2) without the intention to begin assessment promptly is unacceptable.

Greater consistency in the recording of Section 136 is needed. Unacceptable delays in completing an assessment and gaining access to an appropriate placement still occur. Purchasers should consider the desirability of locating places of safety in mental health units.

Most Trusts now have written Section 17 leave policies, but lapses in practice are widespread. Procedures for action when patients go absent without leave need tightening.

Patients' entitlements under the Act to assessments that include examination by two doctors, one who is approved and one who is familiar with the patient, are too often unfulfilled. The Commission strongly recommends that the Department of Health, the Royal Colleges of Psychiatrists and General Practitioners review the implementation of HSG(96)3 and put forward proposals to improve the situation.

3 Admission and Detention

3.1 Admission Trends

Informal psychiatric admission is no different in principle from entering hospital for medical or surgical treatment. Compulsory detention and treatment for mental disorder, when this is necessary for the health or safety of the patient or the protection of others, is authorized and regulated by the Mental Health Act. An application, addressed to an NHS psychiatric unit or Registered Mental Nursing Home, has to be made on a statutory form by an Approved Social Worker (ASW) or by the patient's 'nearest relative', although the former choice is usually considered preferable. The application must be supported by two medical recommendations, at least one from a practitioner 'approved' by the Secretary of State (under Section 12 of the Act) as having special experience in the diagnosis and treatment of mental disorder. Where practicable, one of the recommendations should be from a doctor with prior knowledge of the patient, most likely the patient's GP.

Applications are for assessment up to 28 days (Section 2) or for treatment up to 6 months (Section 3). In cases of urgent necessity, a recommendation by just one medical practitioner (Section 4) suffices for admission up to 72 hours to enable an assessment to be completed. A minority of detained patients are admitted under Part III of the Act from the courts or prison.

Shortcomings in conforming to these procedures and to the supplementary guidance in the Code of Practice are described in this and subsequent chapters.

3.1.1 Number of Admissions

There has been a steady increase in admissions under the Act in recent years. Over the 5 years up to 1994/5, the total number admitted to NHS hospitals in England (excluding High Security Hospitals) increased by 18% to 270,100 per year. In the same period, formal admissions under the Act increased by 53% to 26,100 per year. Furthermore, the rate of increase accelerated. In the years from 1984 to 1989-90, the average increase per annum in formal admissions was 5%, but in the subsequent 5 year period, this increased to 9% per annum (Dept. of Health, 1996a). There are signs that this may now be levelling off, in that the figures for 1995/6 show relatively small increases from the previous year for both formal and informal admissions (Dept. of Health, 1997a)[1].

Admissions under Part II of the Act account for nearly all the increase; changes in admissions via courts and prisons, under Part III of the Act, are small in comparison, as can be seen from the table below. There has, however, been an increase in prison transfers to hospital (via Sections 47 and 48) which have increased to 689, more than double what it was 5 years ago.

Mental Health Act Admissions for England (Dept. of Health, 1997a)

	1989/90	1992/3	1994/5	1995/6
Admissions under Part 11				
Section 2	9573	11535	13195	12572
Section 3	3059	6509	8777	9538
Section 4	1878	1275	1438	1405
Total	14510	19319	23410	23515
From informal to:				
Section 5 (2)		7041	8053	8790
Section 5 (4)		1076	1316	1285
Section 2		2546	2649	2486
Section 3		2275	3724	3669
Total		12938	15742	16230
Part 111				
S.35-38, 47,48	1687	2002	2111	2018

[1] It should be noted that the Department of Health figures refer to the number of times the Act was used when a patient was admitted to hospital from the community and do not include when a patient's legal status was changed from informal to formal. The Commission's hospital profile statistics (see 2.3.2) refer to the number of times the Act was used whether or not the patient was already in hospital. The Department of Health's data includes the uses of the Act in the High Security Hospitals, unlike the Commission's data which does, however, include the uses of the Act in Wales.

The Table shows a changing pattern of use, with a substantial increase in Section 3, a moderate increase in Section 2 and fluctuations in the use of Section 4, an initial fall being followed by a more recent increase.

The increased usage of Section 3 suggests closer adherence to the recommendation in the Code of Practice (5.3a), referred to in the last Biennial Report (3.1). This advises that Section 3 rather than Section 2 should normally be used for patients well known to the clinical team. Another point of good practice is that Section 3 should be rescinded as soon as compulsory powers are no longer needed (in accordance with the Code of Practice advice to discharge from Section at the earliest opportunity). There is a trend, according to one study (Sackett, 1996), for earlier discharge from Section 3, but this does not usually occur until the patient has been allowed to leave hospital. The Commission recommends that the necessity for detention should be reviewed at regular intervals and, if compulsory powers are no longer appropriate, the patient could remain in hospital on an informal basis.

There are some marked local variations in the use of Section 4. The Commission's Hospital Profile statistics for 1995/96 point to a disproportionate number of Section 4 admissions in the North East Thames area (CVT1). There are also reports that difficulties in obtaining a second doctor for admission assessments are causing greater use of Section 4 in some other areas (see 3.5.2).

The increasing proportion of compulsory admissions was supported by the findings of the National Visit (see 1.8). About a third of designated in-patients (32%) on the day of the Visit were detained.

The Commission would like to see further research into the factors, including demographic, geographic and ethnic variables, underlying these statistical trends. An explanation is needed for the considerable rise in compulsory admissions over the past 10 years. Statistical information, supplemented by qualitative analysis of reports from Commission Visits, could help to identify individual units and models of care that are not following general trends. Pointers to good or bad practice might be gleaned from such examples.

Homerton Hospital, City and Hackney NHS Trust: Convenor's comments following Visits in 1996.

While still high, a fall in the number of compulsory admissions has been observed at one hospital. New facilities have opened where it is suggested by senior managers that the falling rate of detentions may be due to the fact that patients are more prepared to stay on an informal basis.

The Commission and the Department of Health Statistical Service intend to collaborate more extensively in the collection and analysis of information about the use of the Mental Health Act.

3.1.2 Receipt and Scrutiny of Section Papers

The forms for making applications and for recording admissions, renewals of detention, and transfers under Part II of the Act are prescribed by the Mental Health (Hospital, Guardianship and Consent to Treatment) Regulations 1983 (as amended). Following a patient's admission these forms should be scrutinised by an authorized officer on behalf of the Hospital Managers. Incorrect or defective applications or medical recommendations can, in certain circumstances, be rectified within 14 days of completion (Section 15).

The Regulations were amended in 1996 and changes were made to some of the statutory forms, clarifying, in particular, the questions to be addressed in medical recommendations. Commission members noted that old forms continued to be used some months after implementation of the new Regulations. Solicitors for one Trust where this happened advised that patients would be unlawfully detained if the unamended forms were used. The Commission sought advice on this issue from the NHS Executive and from its own legal advisors. The NHS Executive's view is that the detention would not be made invalid simply because the amended form is not used, provided that there had been substantial compliance with the requirements of the Act. While the statutory provisions can be correctly reflected in both the old and new forms, the Commission advises the use of the new forms in all cases.

Commission members routinely examine statutory forms and point out errors to the Trusts and independent providers visited.

Coventry Healthcare Trust: Visit 8.3.96

In general, statutory documentation in relation to the currently detained patients was in good order. There were, however, errors of deletion in three Forms 9 (Application by ASW for admission for treatment) and, in one case, in both the medical recommendations (one doctor had failed to delete any category of mental disorder and the other had deleted only one). In another case, one medical recommendation for Section 3 gave the same brief (6 word) statement to justify the choice of mental disorder and the reason why compulsory admission was necessary. This raises the question whether the Hospital Managers had sufficient information to conclude that the grounds for admission were valid and reasonable (Code of Practice 24.7). These issues were discussed with the Patients' Services Manager who agreed to review the scrutiny procedures.

On a subsequent Visit, 27.9.96, Commission members found that legal documentation was subject to both medical and administrative scrutiny and was consequently in good order.

Effective recording systems are needed to alert Responsible Medical Officers (RMOs) in good time before the expiry date of a Section and before certification of consent to medication is required. Commission members have noted occasional failures to complete on time the statutory form to renew detention under Section 3 (Form 30) and to record consent to medication (Form 38).

3.1.3 Rights of Detained Patients

Section 132 requires Hospital Managers to inform detained patients of their legal position and rights under the Act. This includes informing patients about the Commission Visits to their hospital and their right to complain to the Commission (Code of Practice, 14.13d). Unless the patient requests otherwise, the information on rights must also be given to the Nearest Relative.

The giving of information on rights is not always adequately recorded in accordance with the recommendations in the Code of Practice (14.7) and more attention needs to be given to ensuring that the patient understands the information. The Commission recommends that Hospitals and Nursing Homes enhance practice in this area by:

- establishing a system to ensure that the provision of information is properly recorded, including initial attempts that are unsuccessful because the patient is not in a position to understand—(providers may consider introducing a short form for this purpose);

- assigning a designated member of staff to review a patient's understanding of information on rights at intervals during their stay in hospital.

Detained patients are likely to be entitled to vote, if they have a place of residence in the community and are expected to return to that address at the end of the period of detention. Patients should be assisted in exercising their right to vote, told about making a postal vote and helped, where necessary, to complete the required forms (Dept. of Health, 1996c).

The Commission has sought to improve its own dissemination of information to detained patients by the issue of the following 5 leaflets in April 1996:

The Mental Health Act Commission—Leaflet No. 1

Consent to Treatment (Medication)—Leaflet No. 2

Consent to Treatment Electroconvulsive Therapy (ECT)—Leaflet No. 3

How to Make a Complaint—Leaflet No. 4

Neurosurgery for Mental Disorder (Psychosurgery) and the Mental Health Act Commission—Leaflet No. 5 *

* Leaflet No. 5 is relevant for both informal and detained patients, for whom psychosurgery is being considered.

These leaflets should be on display in all hospitals and Registered Mental Nursing Homes accommodating detained patients. They are now also available in 14 foreign languages: Bengali, Chinese (Cantonese, Mandarin), French, German, Gujerati, Hindi, Polish, Punjabi, Somali, Spanish, Tamil, Urdu and Vietnamese. A Commission poster has also been distributed with space for units to insert dates of forthcoming Visits.

3.1.4 Hearing Delays

The administration of Mental Health Review Tribunals (Tribunals) is not within its remit, but the Commission is concerned about hospital policies and practices that have an impact on detained patients' rights and may raise such issues during Visits.

Patients should be made aware of when, according to the Act, they or their nearest relative have the right to apply to a Tribunal. The Act also states when Hospital Managers are required to refer cases to the Tribunal.

Knowing their rights does not always mean patients are able to exercise them fully. The right to apply to a Tribunal can be undermined by delays in holding a hearing, which in some areas are considerable. Commission members have been told of delays of over 12 weeks for unrestricted patients and even longer for restricted patients, particularly those in High Security Hospitals. For patients who believe that the delay is such that they are likely to be discharged before the hearing, an application to a Tribunal may appear an irrelevance.

The Tribunals administration has been faced with an upsurge in applications, reflecting the increase in numbers of detained patients, particularly under Section 3. Patients on Section 2 are better served by the system because of the statutory 7 day time limit for applications to be heard.

Reasons for delays were explored by two Commission members, who examined recent applications by detained patients at four Trusts. The Trusts served inner and outer London populations and mixed urban and rural areas. There were significant delays in forwarding the patients' applications to the Tribunal and further delays in the Tribunal notifying the Trust formally (by standard letter) of the requirement to provide reports within the statutory time periods (Tribunal Rules 6 (1)). It was difficult to see any justification for these administrative delays. Only in one case did a Tribunal exercise its powers under the Regulations to speed up the hearing process. Automatic referrals at statutory intervals by Managers on behalf of patients were particularly poorly processed. One such application was made 3 months after its due date.

The time between the notification and the date set for a hearing was such that reports from RMOs and social workers were often available in advance. It appeared that tardiness in providing statutory reports did not contribute substantially to the overall delays in hearing applications from these Trusts. However, in one case, the Tribunal adjourned proceedings and gave directions that the RMO and social worker should be present at the reconvened hearing. Most patients had legal representation, but efforts made by them to expedite proceedings had little effect.

Patients are not always offered access to the Law Society's panel of solicitors with expertise in mental health law. This list should be available on the wards. Some hospitals keep a limited list, of their own, of solicitors who are regularly called upon. Where there are no local solicitors on the Law Society's list this may be unavoidable, but it can give patients the impression that these solicitors are not fully independent of the hospital. It should be made clear to all patients that they can be represented before Tribunals, free of charge, under the legal aid scheme.

There has been an increase in the number of applications for Hospital Managers' Reviews, probably prompted by the difficulty in gaining quick access to Tribunals. This has led to a corresponding increase in waiting time for these applications, sometimes as much as 6 weeks.

The Bethlem and Maudsley NHS Trust: Visit 2.12.96

At the Visit to the Maudsley Hospital, it was noted that there were possible delays of 6 weeks for the granting of Managers' Hearings. Thirty applications were still outstanding at the time of the Visit. The explanation offered suggested that there had been great difficulty in finding a time to suit both the clinical team members and the Managers. Four Managers were being trained. The Commission recommended that it might be necessary to increase further the available Managers to meet the problem and reduce the delay.

Doncaster Healthcare NHS Trust: Visit 8.11.96

There was difficulty in meeting the rising number of requests for Managers' Hearings and applications were being restricted to Tribunals only. The Commission advised that patients have a right to ask the Managers to review their detention and the Managers should conduct Reviews to deal with these cases. Not all patients who want to be discharged from Section want their case referred to a Tribunal. The two hearings are different and not interchangeable. Patients have a right to both.

Some Trusts have responded to the increased demand by appointing additional Panel Members to share the workload and make the system more efficient:

> **Bexley Hospital, Oxleas NHS Trust: Visit 9/10.9.96**
>
> Commission members commended the implementation of a new system for Managers' Hearings which was working well. There had been an increase in hearings over the last year. At the time, applications to Tribunals by patients detained under Section 3 and Section 37 were being delayed up to four months.

At present, the delays are such that many Section 3 patients are discharged well before they have access to a Tribunal hearing. If improved procedures for informing patients of their rights encourage more applications to Tribunals, swifter access will be needed if delays are not to worsen. The Secretary of State for Health has announced (Press Release 96/2/96) that action is being taken to improve the administrative support for Tribunals and reduce delays. The next edition of the Code of Practice is likely to include guidance on deadlines for hospital staff to provide reports to Tribunals.

The Secretary of State for Health has also announced his intention to abolish the power of Managers to discharge detained patients. The existence of two completely separate systems for patients to obtain a review of their detention is considered to create confusion and duplication of effort. On the other hand, Managers' Hearings provide an additional and sometimes speedier opportunity for patients to put their case to a body in more continuous contact with their situation. Managers, however, may not have the same degree of experience and expertise as Tribunals. In 1996, at the request of the Secretary of State, the Commission convened a Working Group comprising of representatives of the National Association of Health Authorities and Trusts, the NHS Trust Federation and the Royal College of Psychiatrists to consider the adequacy of the current guidance to Managers about Reviews. The recommendations made in the Working Group's Report (Dept. of Health, 1996) have been included in the suggested amendments to the Code of Practice.

3.1.5   Options for the Admission of Adolescents

The Mental Health Act has no age limitation with regard to detention of the mentally disordered, but for young persons there are alternative means, under the Children Act 1989, for providing secure accommodation and, in some circumstances, compulsory treatment. Amongst the recommended changes to the Code of Practice is more extensive guidance about the choice.

The best interests of the young person should always be paramount, with attempts made to select the least restrictive and supposedly least stigmatising option consistent with effective care and treatment. Whilst making specific provisions for overriding refusal of treatment for mental disorder, the Mental Health Act also affords safeguards, including the availability of Second Opinions, the right to apply for review by a Tribunal or by Hospital Managers, the right to communicate with the Mental Health Act Commission, the right to after-care and the provisions for consultation with the nearest relative. These are particularly relevant where there is serious psychiatric disorder requiring specific treatments. Where the main concern is for containment while self-harming and other behavioural disturbance is brought under control, an Order under the Children Act may be preferable. The choice also rests on the point of time at which the safeguards should operate—before or after the decision to detain. If before, the Children Act should be used, as it provides the opportunity for the arguments about the need for compulsory admission to be tested in court. But if immediate action is necessary, the Mental Health Act may be preferable with the decision subject to subsequent review.

3.2 Doctors' Holding Powers: Section 5(2)

The Commission's Hospital Profile statistics show a total of 10,600 detentions under Section 5(2) in England and Wales in 1995/6, but with wide variation between units, some hospitals using it for a high proportion of their patients, others using it minimally. A ratio of more than one implementation of Section 5(2) to every four admissions on Sections 2 or 3 would be unusually high. Thameside Community Healthcare Trust reported a ratio of 29:107 for the year ending 31 March 1996.

A high usage of Section 5(2) is not in itself an indication of misuse, it may simply reflect the nature of the patient intake. However, one factor that might contribute to such usage is a desire to avoid the use of compulsion at the point of admission and treat patients in the least restrictive circumstances possible. While well-intentioned, this may not always be appropriate, as the application of a Section soon after informal admission can leave patients surprised and resentful and increase the likelihood of complaints about loss of freedom (see also 9.4). Too frequent usage may also have the effect of blurring the distinction between informal and detained patients, causing all patients to feel under duress. The Commission will continue to monitor the use of this Section closely.

The Sixth Biennial Report drew attention to an unacceptably high proportion of detentions under Section 5(2) in which assessments are delayed or the time limit allowed to expire without any record of assessment having begun. This does not comply with guidance in the Code of Practice (8.1.b) that "when it is invoked the patient should be assessed as speedily as possible". When it is decided, before an assessment is completed, that detention is no longer necessary, the patient should be discharged at that point and the Section not left to lapse at the end of 72 hours. Many Trusts have continued to audit this Section, encouraged by the Commission, and a general improvement in standards has occurred. However, there are still inconsistencies. Some ASWs have complained to Commission members about being informed at the last moment of the need to complete an assessment or, on occasion, not being informed at all.

Warley Hospital, Barking, Hackney and Brentwood Community Healthcare NHS Trust: Visit 18/19.4.96

One case was noted where a Section 5(2) was allowed to lapse and then, one hour later, the patient was put on a Section. In another instance a patient was not assessed until 15 minutes before the expiry of the 72 hour limit. Commission members also noted comments from Social Services about late notification of Section 5(2) detentions. The Commission recommended monitoring of the use of Section 5(2).

Northern Devon Healthcare Trust: Visit 16.1.97

Very high usage of Section 5(2) was noted, the statistics provided by the Trust indicating it having been applied to over a third of the detained patients. In a high proportion of cases Section 5(2) continued the full 72 hours without the patient being assessed as needing detention under the Act. One patient had been placed on a Section 5(2) at 16.15 hrs. on a Friday and again at 19.15 hrs. on the following Monday; that is within 3 hours of the lapse of the previous application of the Section. The Commission advised that consecutive applications of Section 5(2) are uncommon and hardly ever necessary if assessments are carried out promptly. It was also noted at this Visit that during 1996 a total of 7 patients had been placed in seclusion while on Section 5(2).

Other misuses of Section 5(2) have been noted, for instance the administration of treatment without consent before completion of the assessment. Section 5(2) has also been used on occasion as an aid to the management of transient disturbance, with no intention to convene a full assessment immediately.

3.3   Section 136

It is difficult to quantify the use of this Section, which empowers the police to arrest persons in a public place who appear to be mentally disordered and to convey them to a place of safety for psychiatric assessment and the making of any necessary arrangements for the patient's treatment and care. There are no comprehensive national statistics and no standard system for recording. The Commission's Hospital Profile statistics record 1,899 admissions under Section 136 in 1995/6, with considerable geographic variation. However, these figures give an incomplete picture since they mainly record Section 136 assessments taking place in mental health facilities, whereas in some areas most Section 136 assessments are carried out in police stations.

In inner urban areas, with a high incidence of deprivation, the police are more likely to encounter disordered behaviour requiring the use of Section 136. Unfortunately, these are the areas in which health and social services tend to be overstretched and where finding places for acutely disturbed patients is unusually difficult. A Revolving Doors Agency (1995) survey in inner London found that 'mental health cases' averaged 2.3% of all arrests and 0.76% involved Section 136. Although the places of safety were defined as the local hospital, most were taken to police stations and of these almost 40% were discharged without a proper assessment and received no care.

The report of the Inquiry (Ritchie, 1994) into the treatment of Christopher Clunis recommended the standardisation of documentation used in Section 136 cases. Consideration is being given by the Home Office to more rigorous recording of information and the production of national statistics, which would assist monitoring locally and nationally.

The circumstances leading to arrest under Section 136 can be of clinical significance, but this is not always recorded in the documentation reaching the admitting hospital. Sometimes Commission members find no explicit reference, in clinical notes, that an admission has come about through a Section 136 assessment.

There has, however, been steady improvement in practice relating to Section 136. Many areas now have effective liaison groups, linking health, police and social services, to oversee the operation of the Act, including Section 136. In some areas the time taken to initiate and complete assessments and to secure a bed for those being admitted to hospital is monitored. Such liaison groups provide a forum for resolution of issues such as responsibility for conveyance, provision for those not admitted to hospital yet needing some support and the role of the police if a violent patient needs to be sent to a distant hospital. Nevertheless, problems still occur in some places, with disputes over transport and waiting time for police at hospitals.

It is generally recognised that a cell in a noisy custody department in a busy police station is not an ideal environment in which to assess the mentally disturbed, but other considerations, such as accessibility of the location and the absence of a viable alternative, sometimes means that they have to be used. Concerns about violence by individuals brought to hospitals under Section 136 are voiced with increasing frequency. Accident and Emergency Departments are sometimes used, but these are busy places with obvious drawbacks. A number of Trusts have provided dedicated places of safety for Section 136 assessments at hospitals. Once established, these appear to work well. Many units, however, resist providing accommodation on grounds of expense, demands on staff and insecure environments, while some police forces prefer not to have to bring patients to a hospital where they may have a protracted wait for the patient to be assessed. Nevertheless, the Commission continues to recommend that clear preference should be given, whenever practicable, to the location of places of safety in mental health premises. Purchasers should bear this in mind, especially when plans for the relocation of hospital units in new premises are under consideration.

The use of police cells as places of safety is particularly unfortunate when, following assessment, a patient has to wait over a weekend because of the difficulty of finding a bed.

Gwent NHS Trust: May 1996

The Commission was informed by a consultant psychiatrist that, one Friday evening, a patient, well known locally and suffering a recurrence of manic depressive illness, was brought to a police station under Section 136. He had cut his wrist, threatened arson and been violent towards a police officer. A Section 3 assessment was completed. Nurses at the local psychiatric unit advised that the patient was unsuitable for admission on account of his aggression. Two other units were approached, but both were full and another two would not admit a patient without prior assessment during weekday working hours. In the absence of any prospect of admission before the following Monday, the patient had to be treated in the cells, where he remained overnight. A nurse from the local unit attended and the patient was persuaded to take oral medication. Fortunately, he settled sufficiently to be admitted to the local unit the following day.

Inevitably, Section 136 assessments are likely to be needed urgently at awkward times. Difficulties in obtaining access, out-of-hours, to Approved Social Workers, GPs and Section 12 approved doctors can mean delay. Where no other doctor who has previous acquaintance with the patient, or who is Section 12 approved, is available to provide the second recommendation, one from a Forensic Medical Examiner could be sought. Resort to the provisions of Section 4 should be for genuine emergencies only (see 3.5.2).

When police bring someone to hospital under Section 136 they sometimes use physical restraints, including handcuffs, not normally applied to patients. Concerns have also been raised about the use of CS gas or spray, the short and longer term effects of which on people with mental health problems are uncertain.

At a meeting with Dorset Social Services in May 1996 it was learned that a male patient had been admitted recently to St. Anne's Hospital, Poole, under unusual circumstances. Police, using a Section 135 warrant, entitling them to enter the man's house, had done so and then used CS spray to immobilise him. No doctor was present and the ASW was outside the home when the spray was used. The Commission questioned the appropriateness of the use of CS spray, especially when indoors.

Somerset Social Services Department: Visit 12.3.97

A former patient, well-known to the service, failed to continue treatment and was felt to be neglecting himself and so a decision was made to undertake a full mental health assessment. The patient refused entry and a warrant was obtained under Section 135 of the Mental Health Act. Entry was effected by a police constable accompanied by an ASW and a psychiatrist. After some discussion the patient declined admission to hospital and picked up a knife. The policeman radioed for assistance and when more police arrived, CS spray was used on the patient. Understandably, this action gave rise to considerable concern to the involved agencies. Some ASWs felt that the use of CS spray had such a profound effect on the client that a full assessment could not be adequately undertaken. Further discussions are to be undertaken by the involved agencies.

3.4   Authorization of Leave

Section 17 of the Act requires the RMO to authorize personally any leave granted to a detained patient to go off the hospital grounds for any length of time, however short. Periods of leave can be brief, for example just long enough for a stroll to a nearby shop, or extended over weeks or months in order to test a patient's ability to cope with living in the community.

The maximum length of time to which a patient can remain subject to Section 17 leave has been modified by the Mental Health (Patients in the Community) Act 1995. Since April 1st 1996, unrestricted patients may be given leave for as long as they remain liable to detention; that is for up to six months or one year; (the previous limit was 6 months for all patients). Within the limits of the current authority to detain, the RMO retains responsibility for the patient. The Consent to Treatment provisions and the power to recall the patient to hospital continue to apply while the patient is on leave in the community. There has been insufficient time since its implementation to comment on the impact of longer Section 17 leaves. The Commission intends to give more consideration to any issues arising from the change (i.e. what constitutes good practice, how should it be monitored), when it reviews its Practice Note 4 on *Issues Surrounding Sections 17 and 18 of the Mental Health Act*.

The management changes within the NHS, where it is now possible for different Trusts to manage different units on the same hospital site, has given rise to queries as to what constitutes hospital grounds for the purposes of Section 17 leave. The Commission's view is that if the land and buildings still constitute one hospital, albeit managed by different Trusts, Section 17 leave is not necessary for the patient to move from one part of the hospital to another, but each Trust needs to obtain its own legal advice about its particular circumstances.

The Commission's concerns about the implementation of Section 17 were extensively reported in the Sixth Biennial Report (9.4). An improvement in standards has been observed on Commission Visits. Most Trusts now have written policies and procedures about its use.

Mid-Cheshire Hospitals NHS Trust: Visits 10.5.96 and 7.11.96

At the May Visit the Trust was commended for its pilot scheme on Ward 21A, whereby patients are involved at an early stage in discussions about leave arrangements. At the November Visit the Trust was further commended for the introduction of a checklist for home leave assessments and a home leave planning form.

Blackburn, Hyndburn and Ribble Valley Healthcare NHS Trust: Visit 16/17.1.97

Following criticism at an earlier Visit about the forms used for Section 17 leave, which omitted details of destination and conditions of leave, Commission members noted the use of revised and improved leave forms.

Examples of lapses that have been found to occur include:

no form or record of leave

unlawful delegation of RMO authority

conditions for leave not specified

precise return time unspecified

too much latitude allowed to junior staff when to implement leave

no evidence of multi-disciplinary consultation or leave being incorporated into the care plan

inadequate consultation with relatives or carers about leave

assignment of escort duties to relatives and others who are not officers of the Trust, without first obtaining authorization from the managers (Section 17 (3)).

The Code of Practice (20.5) states that a written copy of the conditions of leave should be given to the patient, to any appropriate relatives/friends and to any professional carers in the community who need to know. This important advice is not often implemented.

Leave forms need to be clear, fully completed, properly authorized and immediately accessible to staff on duty so that there can be no confusion about leave status when a patient asks to go out.

> ### Riverside Mental Health NHS Trust: Visit 19.9.96
>
> At the Henry Rollin Unit, Horton Hospital, Commission members noted the continued use of different forms, apparently for ground parole, short leave and extended leave respectively, but used inconsistently. Some forms were signed by junior doctors, not the RMO. The practice of the RMO signing blank forms in advance (in case leaves have to be rescheduled) is unsatisfactory. Where there is a Section 41 Restriction Order and a Home Office directive about what periods and conditions of leave are allowed, it is particularly important to monitor adherence closely. The leave form of one patient granted escorted leave by the Home Office gave no particulars of escorting arrangements, destinations or review procedures.

Lapses in practice in the operation of Section 17 appear more prevalent in some independent Mental Nursing Homes where some RMOs and nursing staff are still deficient in their knowledge of the correct procedures.

Findings from the National Visit to NHS units also revealed deficiencies in the operation of Section 17. In 29 cases, there was poor recording practice with leave forms either not signed by the RMO or relevant information such as the date of expiry of leave not given.

The National Visit also examined policies covering absence without leave. Most wards (n = 271, 88%) had a relevant policy. A small minority (14) were outdated; some had been drawn up by health authorities which no longer existed or hospitals which had closed. There were five wards with policies dated before 1983. In some instances, different wards within the same Trust had different policies. Sixteen policies were found to be inadequate in terms of the procedure for staff to follow and, in some cases, contact phone numbers, for example of the police, were wrong. Clearly, many Trusts need to update and coordinate their policies, particularly now that new provisions for the return of patients without leave have been introduced, following the implementation of the Mental Health (Patients in the Community) Act 1995.

At the time of the Visit, 32 patients were noted absent without leave. There were 16 other patients where the leave period had expired, but they were not counted as absent without leave, because they were still in touch with staff. In all but one case, ward staff were aware the patients were missing and were following appropriate procedures.

3.4.1 Transfers to other Hospitals

The Sixth Biennial Report referred to the misuse of Section 17 leave to move patients from one hospital to another without implementing a formal transfer under Section 19. Statutory responsibilities remain with the original hospital; thus complications can arise if the patient's liability to detention needs to be renewed, or if consent to treatment forms, which must be signed by the RMO from the first hospital, need to be modified. Since these comments were made, Guidance has been issued (Dept. of Health, 1996g) recommending that, where a patient is to move from one hospital to another, he or she should be transferred at the outset under Section 19 of the Act. The Commission has noted occasional instances where this recommendation has been ignored. For example, some patients have been moved to Regional Secure Units from Ashworth Hospital for extended periods under Section 17. Another example concerned a patient, presenting challenging behaviour, who was transferred to a High Security Hospital under Section 17. The RMO from the Hospital which originally admitted the patient under Section did not wish to be involved, which made care and treatment of the patient more difficult.

Sometimes the use of Section 17 to effect transfers remains preferable.

> **North Lakeland Healthcare NHS Trust: Visit 8.1.97**
>
> A patient detained under Section 3 needed to go to a local hospital for medical investigations. The Commission members felt that in this case, despite general advice to use Section 19 for transfers, Section 17 seemed more appropriate in view of the receiving hospital's inability to cater for the psychiatric and legal requirements of a detained patient and the limited period of care needed. The attention of the Trust was drawn to advice in HSG (96) 28 and the discussion in Jones (1996 at 1.116).

3.5 The Role of General Practitioners

3.5.1 Knowledge of the Mental Health Act

GPs, with knowledge of their patient's background, personality, medical history and social circumstances, have a crucial role to play in the implementation of various aspects of the Act, especially assessment prior to admission. In December 1996, the Commission issued a Guidance Note, *GPs and the Mental Health Act,* which outlines the three main areas with which GPs need to be conversant:

- the assessment of a patient for possible compulsory admission;

- general issues relating to detained patients (the Consent to Treatment provisions and the function of the Nearest Relative);

- post-discharge action.

3.5.2 Availability of GPs

Medical recommendations for compulsory admission (except for Section 4—cases of urgent necessity) must include a recommendation from a doctor approved by the Secretary of State (under Section 12 of the Act). The second recommendation should be from a practitioner who knows the patient, normally the GP. If this is not practicable, then it is desirable (Code of Practice, 2.25) that the second recommendation should also be made by a Section 12 approved doctor.

The Commission has received reports from different parts of England and Wales, where GPs have experienced difficulties in responding to requests to provide second medical recommendations, particularly for assessments of patients already admitted informally to a hospital outside the GP's catchment area or for assessments out of hours.

The NHS (General Medical Services) 1992 Regulations specify that a GP is not obliged to visit a patient at a place outside the practice area. Nor is it mandatory, under their terms of service, for GPs to assess patients for the purposes of providing a medical recommendation under Section 2 or Section 3 of the Act. However, it is good practice and clearly desirable that, in all cases where it is practicable, the GP undertakes the assessment. Unfortunately, the Commission continues to hear of occasional instances where GPs decline to participate in the assessment of their own patients. The following example illustrates the type of difficulty which can arise when GPs do not make themselves available.

A letter to the Commission from an ASW described the response from a patient's GP, practicing in a neighbouring borough, when requested to assess a person brought to hospital on a Section 136. The GP refused to come to the unit, stating categorically that he was "not contractually obliged" to attend there for an assessment under the Act, apparently because the unit was out of his area. This was particularly unhelpful because the lady concerned was totally unknown to all the hospital staff, was in a distressed and dishevelled state and unable to give much detail or account of herself.

Problems in obtaining second medical recommendations occur, out of hours, when GP deputising services or 'on-call co-operatives' are employed and the doctor on duty has no prior knowledge of the patient. If a doctor who knows the patient cannot be obtained, it may be difficult to find a replacement doctor who is approved under Section 12 (see below).

It has been argued that, in such circumstances, a Section 4 emergency application for temporary admission for up to 72 hours, on a single medical recommendation, may be the preferred option. It avoids long delays (especially undesirable if the prospective patient is being held in a police cell for assessment under Section 136) and it allows time for the GP or an adequate substitute to be obtained. In Oxford (see 3.6) this procedure appears to have become a matter of policy rather than a response to a true emergency. However, compulsory admission, even for a short assessment, is a traumatic event for the patient and more so if it occurs out of hours, particularly during the night. It remains the Commission's view that anybody being considered for admission from the community under Part II of the Act should ordinarily be entitled to rely on the safeguard of being assessed by two doctors rather than one. The use of Section 4 should be restricted to cases of urgent necessity, where delay in obtaining a second doctor would be undesirable.

The Commission is aware of other proposals by GP deputising services or co-operatives in different parts of England and Wales for operational procedures which could have the effect of short-circuiting the Code of Practice guidance. For example, one GP co-operative proposed that the medical recommendation could be signed and left behind without any consultation with the social worker or psychiatrist. The Commission would be most concerned if such developments led to practices which served the expediency of the deputising service rather than the interests of patients.

3.6   Access to Section 12 Doctors

Obtaining the services of two doctors to carry out medical assessments for compulsory admission under the Act generally falls to Approved Social Workers (ASWs) and, not infrequently, it proves very difficult to locate an approved doctor because of their limited availability.

Extract from memo of 5th November 1996 to colleagues from a Mental Health Care Manager in Reading.

Availability of GPs from West Berkshire to assess patients at Fairmile Hospital under the Mental Health Act

I am aware that you may have heard the recent discussion during the final session of the Mental Health Act Commission's visit to Fairmile Hospital on 11.10.96 regarding the above issue ...

The most recent list of Medical Practitioners Approved under Section 12 (2) of the Mental Health Act was published by the Health Authority on 18.05.95. There are 82 names on this list, of which 22 have an address in East Berkshire, a further 24 are based in Broadmoor Hospital, 7 are no longer practising as Approved Doctors, 2 are based at HMP Brixton and Holloway respectively and one in Surrey. Of the 26 remaining doctors, 19 are based at

Fairmile Hospital, 3 specialise in child and adolescent psychiatry, one in learning disability and one is available only in the evenings. This leaves two Section 12 doctors who may be available, both of whom are GPs with busy practices in the Reading area and are Police Surgeons which is another call on their time...

The Code of Practice, paragraph 2.10 states that "it is important to emphasise that where an ASW is assessing a person for possible admission under the Act he has overall responsibility for coordinating the process of assessment...". I do not think that the term 'co-ordination' extends to the ASW making upwards of 14 telephone calls in order to seek out a doctor who is prepared to make a second medical assessment under the Act.

The difficulty ASWs experience in obtaining the services of Section 12 doctors is particularly acute in areas where hospital-based Section 12 doctors do not make themselves available for community assessments, or in areas where the majority of Section 12 doctors are employed by the same Trust and may decline to become involved on the grounds that independent assessments cannot be guaranteed. It is only when doctors are on the staff of the same hospital that they are, in fact, debarred.

A further concern for the Commission is the number of admission recommendations given by doctors who are neither Section 12 approved nor have previous acquaintance with the patient. Problems in obtaining the requisite recommendations may also lead to inappropriate use of Section 4.

Oxfordshire Mental Healthcare NHS Trust: Visit 24.2.97

Commission members were informed that Forensic Medical Examiners had withdrawn from Mental Health Act assessment work in early 1996, GP deputising services were unwilling to undertake it and only one of the small number of community-based Section 12 approved doctors was readily available. From 1 October 1996 senior registrars had declined to provide the second medical recommendation where both the Section 12 doctors worked for the Trust, albeit at separate hospitals. Increased use of Section 4 was anticipated. Commissioners were told that over the 8 years up to 31 July 1996 it had been used on only 4 occasions in Oxfordshire. During the last 7 months, up to 24 February 1997, it had been used 7 times. Of these 7 people 4 had been held at the police station and reference was made in the documentation to the unavailability of GPs or Forensic Medical Examiners to make an assessment under the Act. It was clear that sometimes Section 4 was being used other than in genuine emergencies, which is contrary to the Act.

The shortage of available Section 12 doctors from the community meant that reliance was placed on the goodwill and co-operation of others. The lack of Section 12 doctors independent of the Trust compounded the problem. The Visit Report concluded that the

> Commission would like to hear from Oxfordshire Health Authority what steps have been taken to recruit Section 12 doctors and to make the task more attractive to them.

The appointment of doctors under Section 12 is the responsibility of Health Authorities, the Secretary of State having delegated his power of approval. Guidance has been issued (HSG (96)3) requiring them "to take steps to encourage suitably qualified medical practitioners, including general practitioners and those working in the prison medical service, to apply for approval". One Health Authority has been identified, within each NHSE regional office area, to take the lead role in Section 12 doctor issues. The issue is not merely one of appointing a sufficient number, but ensuring availability. Health Authorities, together with the Royal Colleges of Psychiatrists and General Practitioners, need to consider ways of increasing the availability of Section 12 doctors. Suggestions have been made to increase fees paid to GPs and to make the participation of Section 12 approved doctors on a duty rota part of the requirement for consultant appointments.

3.7   The Role of Approved Social Workers

ASWs have overall responsibility for managing the process of compulsory admission. One of these duties is to ensure the documentation is correct.

> **Northern Devon Healthcare Trust: Visit 16.1.97**
>
> The administrator reported that almost half of all statutory documents have to be returned for the rectification of errors under Section 15 of the Act. Although mostly minor faults, this level of errors reflects poorly on the care with which doctors are completing their recommendation forms and also on ASWs, who should be checking them as well as their own application forms before admission.

The concerns consistently raised with the Commission by ASWs are as follows:

- difficulties in securing the services of Section 12 doctors and GPs for assessments under the Act;

- difficulty in obtaining beds for patients who need urgent admission (particularly acute in some parts of London) - although a medical responsibility, in practice ASWs are often left to deal with the problem;

- delay in being informed about assessments urgently required for people subject to Section 5(2) or Section 136 procedures;

- concerns about the detention of mentally disturbed people in police cells as a result of the continuing use of police stations as places of safety for assessments under Section 136.

Some of these difficulties appear to arise from organisational problems.

Greenwich Hospital: Oxleas NHS Trust, Visit 16/7.9.96

Commission members were disquieted to learn that there was still uncertainty about the Social Services Department's policy regarding the 'out of hours' social worker's responsibility for assessments under Section 5(2) and the hospital's perception that social workers were not prepared to attend over the weekend. There was still uncertainty as to whose responsibility it was to co-ordinate the assessment procedure. Liaison with the patient's GP was frequently delegated to ward nursing staff. From the available statistics, there was an implication that assessments for Section 5(2) were taking close to the three day time limit.

Difficulties in recruiting sufficient numbers of ASWs persist in some areas. This can lead to individual ASWs having to carry out more assessments than may be desirable or being unable to attend Section 117 meetings.

Blackdown Hospital: Dorset Community NHS Trust, Visit 4.7.96

Professional attendance at multi-disciplinary meetings is adequate, but could be improved. Social workers, in particular, have difficulty in attending, because for some time the Department is said to have been seriously under-staffed, so that the service is largely one of crisis intervention. Duties of a preventative or supportive nature are being sidelined. There is a shortage of ASWs in West Dorset and delays on call-out can be unacceptably long.

In response to these comments, the Social Services Department indicated that, due to a difficult period of staff vacancies, sickness and holidays, the normal social work establishment had been reduced and high risk work was being prioritised. They drew attention to their significant investment in mental health in recent years.

The purchaser-provider split within Social Services has resulted in organisational divisions which are not always easy for service users and staff from other organisations to understand. Some ASWs are located in assessment and commissioning teams, while others are integrated into Community Mental Health Teams and have a caseload of people to whom they provide community support or care management. Some ASWs fear that their role is being diminished by an increasing concentration on statutory assessment duties. The Commission recommend that Social Services Departments ensure that local arrangements do not prevent their ASWs retaining their expert knowledge of community care resources which help them to carry out Section 13 assessments effectively.

Basic training for ASWs has been strengthened by the Central Council for Training and Education in Social Work, which has introduced a quality assurance framework for the approval, review and inspection of ASW programmes in England and Wales (Central Council, 1996). This includes a requirement that training programmes have a formal system in place for assessing whether social workers have acquired the specified competences. Despite some early local difficulties in securing approval for some of the training programmes, the system now appears to be working well. The Commission has noticed improvements in ASWs' grasp of legal issues.

ASWs can only be approved for five years in the first instance. ASWs who have been on refresher courses have given mixed feedback. The Commission would like to see more consistency in courses and attention being paid to the criteria for re-approval of ASWs by local authorities. Possessing the power to deprive a person of their liberty is a heavy responsibility. It is crucial that ASWs receive continuing departmental and peer group support. This does not always happen.

> **Lambeth Healthcare NHS Trust & Social Services Department: Visit 1.4.96**
>
> ASWs usually make Mental Health Act assessments alone, albeit with the expectation of meeting colleagues from other agencies. They are equipped with mobile phones, but these are unreliable. There are no formal debriefing sessions following visits, and although ASWs supposedly meet on a monthly basis, these meetings are poorly attended, offering little opportunity for peer support. At a time of major change and upheaval, it is essential that staff feel supported and the Commission hopes that departmental managers will give their staff every encouragement to meet together on a regular basis.

There have been some joint training enterprises (e.g. on the introduction of supervised discharge) involving Trusts, Local Authorities and other agencies. In some areas these involve service users and carers. The Commission welcomes these developments as they can foster mutual understanding and joint working as well as disseminating knowledge of the Act and the Code of Practice.

3.8 Conveyance to Hospital

The Commission is aware of occasional problems, for instance long waits when ambulance services do not give sufficient priority to the conveyance of patients under section, or when police are needed to assist in moving a violent patient. Generally, however, there is good liaison between the various statutory services over assessment, admission and conveyance to hospital. The London Ambulance Service (1996) has produced guidelines setting out clearly the respective roles and responsibilities of ASWs, ambulance staff and police. There are good jointly agreed policies in some areas, but the Commission would like to see that all Trusts and Social Services have an agreed policy with ambulance services and police. This is all the more important now that there is a power to convey patients under Supervised Discharge.

Chapter **4**

Hospital Issues

Summary

The same problems of high bed occupancy cited in the last two Biennial Reports continue in many areas, especially in London.

There have been marked improvements in the physical environment in units throughout England and Wales, but there is still wide variation in standards. Conditions in older units planned for closure are often poor.

The level and quality of interaction between nurses and patients is a matter of concern for the Commission. Staffing levels and deployment need to take into account the increasing proportion of patients who are detained and the high number 'at risk' and needing observation. The Commission urges that greater attention is paid to the need for access to a range of therapeutic services as well as adequate daytime activity during a hospital stay.

The Commission recommends as a measure to secure privacy and safety that, wherever practicable, patients' single rooms should be lockable from the inside, but with staff having a master key.

The Commission recommends that the Regulations of the Registered Homes Act 1984 should be amended to specify compliance with Mental Health Act procedures as a necessary prerequisite for the registration of Mental Nursing Homes to receive detained patients.

There are concerns about detained patients being placed out of district, leading to difficulties in maintaining home contact and coordinating Section 117 after-care meetings. Innovative solutions should be sought to facilitate multi-agency agreement of Section 117 after-care plans, including prior to Tribunal Hearings or Managers' Reviews, for patients placed out of district.

Medium and High Secure Units should provide environments which have the physical facilities and activity programmes (including at weekends and holiday periods) to give adequate quality of life and stimulation to patients who often have to reside there for a number of years.

There are some inordinate delays in implementing transfers from High Security Hospitals. Efforts by Consultants to expedite procedures might have an influence and more effective communication with patients about their transfer arrangements would be beneficial.

4 Hospital Issues

4.1 Services under Pressure

The same heavy pressure on beds cited in the last two Biennial Reports continues with the following consequences: leave beds are occupied; patients are discharged early; patients may be kept in police cells for one or two days while a bed is found; patients are placed out of district.

The problems are most serious in inner London where bed occupancy rates have been increasing steadily and the threshold for admission has become very high. The proportion of patients detained in inner London hospitals is three times what it is in other inner cities and four times that for England as a whole (Johnson et al 1997).

> **St. Ann's Hospital, Haringey Healthcare NHS Trust: Visits 9.5.96 (unannounced) and 7/8.11.96**
>
> On 9.5.96. extreme bed pressures were reported with occupancy levels as high as 150% and up to 90% of patients detained. Patients were being sent home on leave and attending the hospital on a daily basis.
>
> The Commission Visit Report of 9.5.96 criticised the use of seclusion rooms as bedrooms on the four acute admission wards. The rooms were inadequately ventilated with insufficient privacy. Patients had only a plastic covered mattress on the floor and there was nowhere for them to sit in comfort and nowhere to place their clothes or belongings.
>
> On the next Visit it was noted that an instruction had been issued by the Trust Board that seclusion rooms were not to be used as bedrooms, but it seemed that it was not possible to adhere to the policy, at times, and seclusion rooms were still being used when no other bed could be found for patients who had to be admitted.

City and Hackney Community Services NHS Trust: Visit 19.12.96

Bed occupancy in December was 140%. There was frequent movement between wards; one patient moved 3 times in 11 days. One patient said that he had been given a bed so recently vacated that the linen had not been changed. Bed blocking was exacerbating the problem. On the day of the Visit to Bevan Ward, a locked facility, 6 of the 15 patients there were awaiting transfer to an open ward.

According to the National Visit findings, there were 98 patients for every 100 beds. Once patients on leave had been excluded, this figure fell to 86 patients for every 100 beds. There was considerable variation in levels of bed occupancy, as can be seen in figure 6. On 8% of the wards, there were more patients than designated beds for them.

Figure 6: Percentage of wards by percentage bed occupancy

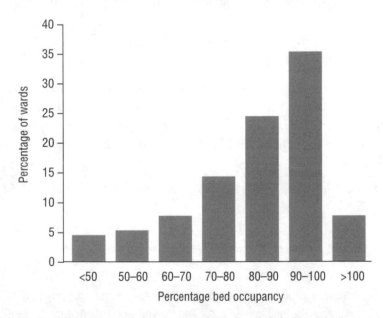

Nb. Chart excludes leave beds

The Commission hears of the problems of high occupancy on many of its Visits. In some areas the pressures are undoubtedly acute, but there could be a number of factors operating. It is important that local planners assess what is happening in their areas. Beds may be taken up by patients placed from other districts. Pressures on the local acute unit are sometimes caused by blockages in other parts of the system resulting from lack of medium secure beds or inadequate community facilities and after-care planning.

The Commission is particularly concerned about patients being placed out of district, as such placements can lead to difficulties in maintaining the continuity of treatment and care required for detained patients. On the one hand, if the placement is brief, it may be unsettling and disruptive; and on the other hand, if it is long-term, there is a risk of loss of contact with the home area (see 4.4.4).

4.2 Therapeutic Environment

A key function of the Commission Visits to hospitals and mental nursing homes is to examine the therapeutic environment. This is of particular importance to detained patients because they are generally unable to exercise choice with regard to the conditions of their stays in hospital. Commission members pay particular attention to the physical environment, staffing levels and quality of care.

4.2.1 Physical Environment

There have been marked improvements in a number of ward environments throughout England and Wales, but a considerable variation in standards has been noted between units.

There are reports of sub-standard units, where wards are described as shabby, scruffy and poorly furnished. Long promised improvements may not materialise because of shortage of money. The conditions and patient mix in older units planned for closure are of particular concern.

Warley Hospital, Barking, Havering and Brentwood Community Healthcare Trust: Visits 18/19.4.96 and 11.10.96

Warley Hospital is subject to substantial reprovision and refurbishment plans, but in the meantime, in spite of very recent efforts to effect improvements, conditions on one block in particular were described by senior managers as "an extremely inhospitable environment to live in". The Commission members recorded, in the October 1996 visit, their extreme disappointment that no progress appeared to have been made in reaching agreement to allocate what were apparently available resources to resolve a problem of such severity and urgency.

Conditions on some other acute admission wards were also poor; problems included inadequate toilet and washing facilities lacking in hygiene and privacy; single rooms poorly furnished with no chairs and no space for personal belongings; poor facilities for making drinks. Staff had made efforts on one or two wards to provide a clean and cheerful environment. The April 1996 Visit reported that staff have raised funds for improvements, which should really be the responsibility of the hospital.

Since these visits, and prior to closure, the Commission has been notified that, in response to the Visit Reports and the Commission members' adverse comments on the environment, monies have been released by North Thames NHS Executive and improvements made to the wards.

St Mary's Hospital, Scarborough and North East Yorkshire Healthcare Trust: Visit 16.7.96

Derwent ward, an acute admission ward, is one of the few facilities left on the St Mary's site. It has become very isolated from the rest of the Trust's services, and the environment is apparently suffering as a result. There has been a reduction in facilities for patients and an inappropriate patient mix. The standard of accommodation and decor is poor. Consequently, many patients are reluctant to accept admission. Given that the accommodation is to be in use until at least 1998, consideration should be given to making temporary improvements.

South Bedfordshire Community Healthcare Trust: Visit 12.1.96

The patient mix on Ward F11 included an undesirably extreme range from 20 to 83 year olds. Only one qualified nurse with the support of one or two unqualified staff was available for 28 patients on this ward. Commission members understood that this situation was a consequence of impending closure, but this is not now expected for some time.

It is sometimes possible to improve conditions, despite planned contraction.

De La Pole Hospital, East Yorkshire Healthcare Trust: Visit 11.11.96

All patients of the Trust were due to be relocated by March 1997. The Commission members were impressed by the efforts made to keep the conditions within the hospital clean and well decorated at a time of retraction and relocation of the service.

Where wards are being refurbished, care needs to be taken to minimise disruption to patients.

St Luke's Hospital, Camden and Islington: Visit 20.9.96 (unannounced)

Noel Harris Ward was being upgraded to become a locked facility for the most seriously ill patients. At the time of the Visit, Commission members found the works programme being undertaken by contractors working around patients and nursing staff. As a consequence the ward was extremely noisy from the continuous use of hammers and drill, the smell of paint (still wet in parts) was offensive and workmen's tools, cabling and equipment were observed in all areas. During the Visit it was discovered that a patient had consumed a quantity of white spirit, obtained from a bottle left by the workmen. Commission members were also present when the fire alarm was set off by smoke from a workman's drill. The fire brigade had been called out on 6 occasions since the work programme began. The chaotic conditions were deemed to be totally untherapeutic.

Second unannounced Visit: 17.10.96

Commission members concluded that many of the issues which had been raised were now either resolved or in process of resolution. It was felt that the Trust was to be commended for the determined efforts it had made to ameliorate the damage and that the experience would not be repeated in the event of future major refurbishments.

The St Luke's Hospital example shows that an unannounced Visit can sometimes both identify a problem and help to secure a resolution.

A detail of the environment, important for the privacy and safety of patients accommodated in single rooms, is the provision of doors that are lockable from the inside but which can be opened by staff with a master key. The Commission recommends the use of this simple arrangement wherever practicable.

4.2.2. Staffing Issues and Patient Activity

The level and deployment of staff, limited interaction with patients, inadequate skill mix and difficulties of recruitment in a number of disciplines are all matters of concern, which have been identified on routine Commission Visits and on the National Visit. Problems in these areas are exacerbated by the pressures of caring for patients who may be difficult to manage on wards with high occupancy. Such conditions are not conducive to a therapeutic environment or to the achievement of a correct balance of tranquility and/or stimulation from staff to match the needs of each individual patient.

Severe shortage of nursing staff is reported at some units with reliance on staff from a nursing bank who may not be familiar with the patients or the therapeutic regime. Difficulty in recruitment for nursing posts is most acute at some Regional Secure Units and Intensive Care Units.

Marlborough House RSU - Milton Keynes Community NHS Trust: Visits of 2.8.96 (unannounced) and 22.11.96

Marlborough House was reported to be experiencing a considerable turnover of staff. The Trust are engaged in assertive recruitment programmes, but recruitment and retention of nursing staff remain problems and nurses are working long hours to maintain cover. At the time of the August 1996 Visit, there was reliance on one or more bank nurses for each shift and admissions had been restricted, so that not all the beds were occupied and the activity programme was minimal with almost nothing planned for the weekend.

However, there has been more success in the recruitment of clinical psychologists and in improving the level of medical staff, which was almost up to a full complement at the time of the November 1996 Visit.

Problems in providing for activity are particularly acute in special care wards (sometimes called intensive care/secure wards). Doors are locked and all or most patients are formally detained. Under such conditions, patients experience severe curtailment of liberty, even though they are not technically secluded. On such wards particular care has to be paid to maintaining standards. For instance, activities which can relieve boredom and feelings of oppressive confinement, such as a walk in fresh air, may be too readily denied on grounds of shortage of staff for escort duties. Zigmond (1995) has made some helpful suggestions for coping in these wards, commenting on the need for close managerial scrutiny, rotation of staff, a multi-disciplinary team, budgets for repair and replacement and at least a minimum level of activity and fresh air.

While particular units have serious staffing problems, the National Visit to acute psychiatric admission and intensive care wards showed that there was one member of nursing staff on duty at the time of the Visit for, on average, 3.3 patients (excluding those on leave). This ratio might be considered adequate, but a more important indicator of quality of nursing care is the level of interaction between nurses and patients.

Extract from ''Report on the Mental Health Act Commission National Visit'' (21.11.96)

A quarter of wards visited (77 wards with 490 staff) were observed to have no staff in contact with patients on the ward. On a further 32% of wards, only one nurse was in contact with patients. Many of the staff in contact with patients were involved in continuous observation of patients at risk of self-harm or violence. If staff involved in continuous contact with 'at risk' patients were excluded, there would be 38% of wards with no staff in contact with patients. Therefore, a significant factor influencing staff contact with patients is the level of 'risk' of self-harm or violence which they feel a patient represents.

It is important to note that, in each ward, one member of staff accompanied the Commission members during the Visit and therefore was not available for patient contact.

Staffing levels need to take into account the increasing proportion of patients who are detained and the high number 'at risk' and needing observation. One or two demanding patients displaying challenging behaviour can easily lead to a relative neglect of others. Direct contact with patients is further limited by the amount of nursing time taken up with administration and case reviews. Staff need to be available and trained to give high priority to engaging with patients in activities and personal discussion. It has to be said that Commission members have on occasion seen nurses apparently interacting with each other rather than with the patients and, as mentioned earlier (see 2.3), 'nurses too busy to talk' was one of the issues frequently brought up by patients themselves.

Fulbourn Hospital, Addenbrookes NHS Trust: Visit 8.3.96 (Unannounced)

It was reported that the number of close observations have created pressure on staffing so that other jobs were being left undone. On Friends Ward, an acute admission ward, at the time of the Visit, 3 patients were on one-to-one observation and 2 on 5 minute observations. There were on duty 2 staff nurses, 1 bank nurse and 3 care assistants.

The dormitories appeared chaotic, beds still unmade at lunchtime, heaps of clothes on beds and floor due to limited personal wardrobe space, ashtrays overflowing and plates left by beds. The tea and coffee making facility in the smoke room was in an unhygienic state with cutlery wrapped in personal clothing left in the sink.

The situation was made more difficult by the layout, which was not conducive to the general observation and monitoring of patients. The Trust was taking steps to improve this and was also considering a contingency budget to cover observation duties.

Commission members have noted that despite many units experiencing increased levels of disturbance demanding skilled nursing care, the proportion of unqualified staff has increased in places. Recruitment problems and efforts to reduce costs appear responsible.

Prestwich Hospital, Mental Health Services of Salford: Visit 7/8.3.96

There was considerable concern about staffing levels at Meadowbrook Hospital, the reliance on bank nurses and the skill balance of staff. Situations could arise where the only qualified nurse on a ward is the bleep holder for the unit who might be called away at any time. Commission members were given to understand that, as nurses move into full-time or permanent posts, there are fewer available to work on the bank and established nurses must therefore increase their overtime work. Staffing levels were particularly problematic on the long-stay wards at Prestwich Hospital. Senior managers were aware of the problem and taking steps to mitigate the effects.

These concerns do not show up in the findings from the National Visit which indicate that 60% of staff are on qualified grades (D and above), representing a reasonably acceptable balance of staffing. Figure 7 gives the total establishment by grade on the wards visited during the National Visit.

Figure 7: Staff grades – National Visit

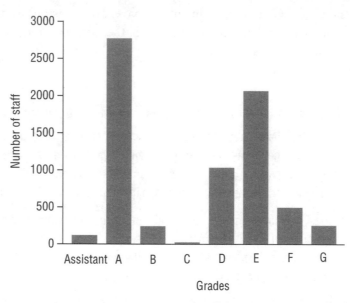

However, as mentioned above, what is most important is how staff are deployed. It is likely that junior and unqualified staff are more often engaged in direct contact with patients, while senior staff with managerial responsibilities are less so.

Many units are also experiencing problems in recruiting psychiatrists, psychologists and occupational therapists.

Langdale Unit, Guild Community Trust: Visits 20/21.7.95, 5.1.96 and 11/12.7.96

It was reported that although the unit was operating as an RSU, it was certainly not staffed as one. There were concerns in January 1996 about the continuing situation of there being only one consultant and the inability to fill the nursing establishment with appropriately qualified staff. Initiatives were being taken to rectify the deficiencies in the clinical psychology service and to recruit another consultant.

The Commission is aware of the particular shortage of forensic psychiatrists and of the difficulty in filling vacant posts. A recent change, which does not apply to the independent sector, requiring consultants to be on the General Medical Council's specialist register before they can take up an appointment, may increase recruitment problems and dependence on locum appointments.

Some in-patient units are losing experienced staff, who are attracted to alternative posts in the independent sector.

St Crispins and Princess Marina Hospitals, Northampton Community Healthcare NHS Trust: Visit 8.8.96

There was concern about psychologists and consultant staff leaving the local Trust to take up posts at nearby St Andrew's Hospital. Commission members had serious doubts about the Trust's ability to deliver an adequate service.

Two of the consultants on one ward were leaving for St Andrew's; another two were locums. The same ward had experienced a recent serious incident of violence, during which repeated attempts to telephone for medical assistance were of no avail. The consultant eventually arrived after the violent patient had been taken away by the police.

It was reported on another ward that Section 17 leave had been granted by a locum RMO and immediately withdrawn by another consultant who was of the opinion that, due to the RMO's unfamiliarity, the risks had been underestimated.

The Commission was pleased to be informed in March 1997 of the successful recruitment of 5.6 consultant psychiatrists, the latest one to start in June 1997, and that the required nursing vacancies had also been filled.

There are continuing problems in filling occupational therapy posts, as was highlighted in the Sixth Biennial Report (page 79) and nurses are being employed to provide an OT type service, but may lack the necessary skills. An insufficiency of nurses, compounded by shortages of occupational and other therapists, can mean that ward activities are substantially curtailed, with patients experiencing high levels of inactivity and boredom.

South Warwickshire Mental Health Services NHS Trust: Visits 22.8.96 and 27.2.97

A 20 bedded acute admission ward was accommodating 21 patients at the time of the Visit and leave beds were in use for urgent admissions. Commission members expressed concern at the limited ward activities due to the loss of a music therapist and the forthcoming departure of the art therapist. By the time of the next Visit, the same problem had arisen on another ward. However, therapy input was deemed good on other wards and nurse staffing levels and skill mix were satisfactory.

Care must be taken not to neglect the needs of older patients for therapeutic and diversional activities.

> **Bolton Hospital NHS Trust: Visit 15.8.96**
>
> Fall Birch Hospital, which caters for the continuing care needs of the elderly, is geographically isolated and remote from the rest of the service and as a result, it appeared to have no input from services such as physiotherapy and OT. The Trust commissioned an Independent Inquiry to review mental health services during December 1996, which confirmed that there was an inadequate psychology and OT input to Elderly Mentally Ill services. The Trust now aims to increase these services and also to improve the environment and accommodation for these patients.

4.3   Registered Mental Nursing Homes

4.3.1   Introduction

Under the Registered Homes Act 1984, Health Authorities register and inspect Nursing Homes on behalf of the Secretary of State. Mental Nursing Homes must be separately registered and may only detain patients under the Mental Health Act if specifically registered to do so. Registered Homes must comply with all the provisions of the Mental Health Act. To assist them with these responsibilities, the Commission issued Practice Note 5, in July 1996, entitled *Guidance on Issues Relating to the Administration of the Mental Health Act in Mental Nursing Homes Registered to Receive Detained Patients.*

The Commission has a statutory duty to visit detained patients in Registered Mental Nursing Homes. The total number of beds is increasing significantly (see 2.2.2) and are situated in Homes which range from large hospitals providing medium secure care to small establishments, where there may only be one or two patients detained under the Act. The Commission is keen to impress on Registering Authorities and the Homes that even though the Homes may be called upon only occasionally to accommodate detained patients, this must not lead to duties and responsibilities under the Act being neglected.

4.3.2   Care in Smaller Mental Nursing Homes

Commission members have reported a wide variation in the standards of care offered in Mental Nursing Homes. While most strive hard to provide a comfortable environment with a range of activities for residents, the obligations laid down in the Act are liable to be ignored or poorly addressed. For instance, it is not unusual to find that the Home holds few, if any, statutory documents relating to the resident's detention under the Act. It then becomes impossible to scrutinise the authority under which a resident is detained. However, at a number of Homes the Commission has found high quality documentation.

Cheadle Royal Hospital: Visit 14.11.96

Documentation was well organised and accessible with clear evidence of medical and administrative scrutiny. The checklist in use is a most useful addition.

Where deficiencies in documentation occur in Homes with generally well-organised procedures, they often relate to Forms 14 and 15, where there is a failure to record correctly the formal admission and the receipt of medical recommendations.

Authorization for treatment for a resident's mental disorder under the Consent to Treatment regulations is not always apparent, either because Form 38 is not in evidence or, more usually, due to irregularities in its completion.

Another issue, highlighted from Commission Visits, is protection of residents' statutory rights. There is only patchy adherence to Section 132, the duty to provide information to patients and ensure that it is understood sufficiently. However, there are examples of good practice. Good use of Section 132 was noted at Ticehurst Clinic, Brighton (November, 1996 Visit) as was the information offered to the sole detained patient at Candle Court Nursing Home in London.

There is a recurrent difficulty with the discharge of Managers' obligations to review detention. Formal arrangements may not be in place or there may be problems of finding suitable, independent candidates to perform the task. There are exceptions, as was noted at a Visit to Grovelands Priory Hospital, Southgate, London (November, 1995), when the unit was commended for its efforts in training Managers under the Act. It was noted that training would be further enhanced by the opportunity to observe how Managers review patient's detention elsewhere.

The Commission regularly seeks to liaise with Health Authorities, who are responsible for registration and inspection, and encourages them to exercise vigilance on matters relating to detained patients. Manchester Health Commission are to be commended for their supplementary guidelines for the registration and conduct of mental nursing homes, which gives a simple checklist of requirements in addition to the general Mental Nursing Home guidance. The Commission routinely sends copies of its Visit Reports to Health Authorities and notifies them when there are particular concerns.

Aaron House Nursing Home: Visit 5.1.96.

A number of deficiencies in Mental Health Act procedures were noted.

There were no copies of any documentation pertaining to one resident detained under Section 3 of the Act, on leave under Section 17. There were also no copies of either a Form 38 or 39 or a Section 17 leave form. It was understood that only escorted leave was permitted. The importance of copies of leave forms being available to those actually detained and consent forms to those giving medication to the detained person was stressed.

There did not appear to be any procedure in place for the receipt or scrutiny of section papers. Only an outdated copy of the Code of Practice was available and there was no specific training in Mental Health Act or Code of Practice issues.

If Managers' Reviews were held, the panel consisted of the person registered as the Home Owner, the Director of Operations and an individual from the local advocacy service. As the panel included an employee of the home, (although not unlawful) it was thought desirable to review the arrangement.

Wirral Health Authority used the report to assist their monitoring and obtained a voluntary agreement that the Home would not admit patients subject to detention under the Act until the Authority were satisfied that proper systems and procedures were in place to meet the statutory responsibilities.

There is no provision under the Registered Homes Act 1984 and its Regulations for Registering Authorities to require that adequate Mental Health Act procedures are in place prior to registration. Failures to adhere to statutory requirements in the care of detained patients generally reflect a lack of knowledge of the Act, rather than a deliberate attempt to bypass it. However, the Commission recommends that the regulations of the Registered Homes Act 1984 be amended, so that registering authorities can withhold or withdraw registration from Mental Nursing Homes to admit detained patients on the grounds of lack of compliance with Mental Health Act procedures. Meanwhile the Commission will continue to draw shortcomings to the attention of NHS purchasers and registering authorities so that standards can be developed and monitored systematically.

4.4 Medium Secure Services

4.4.1 An Expanding Service

There has been a marked expansion in medium secure services during this reporting period (see 10.8.1) in both NHS and independent sectors.

In the NHS sector, new units have been established, such as Wathwood Regional Secure Unit, Rotherham, where the ward environment was described as exemplary in the Report of its first Commission Visit in February 1997. Some units have moved to new large premises (e.g. Crozier Terrace, City and Hackney; Eric Shepherd Medium Secure Unit, Shenley; Humber Lodge Secure Unit, Hull). Other units have expanded significantly such as Three Bridges, West London (now with 81 beds) and Bracton Clinic, Bromley (72 beds). The standard of accommodation in these new or improved units is very high and some are now becoming sizeable institutions.

In the North-West Region, there has been a significant development for those with mental illness and challenging behaviour who require relatively long periods of in-patient care in a secure environment. This group of patients has specialised needs, not feasible to meet on a local basis and so the Regional Office of the NHS Executive has formed a regional network of high dependency beds and set local targets for Health Authorities to develop their own intensive care units and community residential care provision.

North-West Region Development

A network of high dependency units has been established in the North-West. The seven units offer patient care in a secure environment for people with challenging behaviour and enduring mental illness. Each has an identified geographic area within which it has responsibility to provide care, but in theory any of them can be accessed by residents of the North-West. The service is purchased solely by Health Authorities in the North-West and extra contractual referrals are not accepted. This has caused a difficulty for patients currently in Ashworth Hospital, who are not local residents, but wish to be transferred to a unit in the North West. In principle, they cannot gain access to the network, despite agreement by their responsible Health Authority or Social Service Department to fund such a placement.

Common referral, admission and discharge criteria and protocols have been established, as have a set of principles covering philosophy of care, quality of environment and staffing levels. It is intended that patients will remain in the high dependency units for about a year, but they should not remain longer than two years. Patients whose length of stay is likely to be of less than 3 months duration will not be admitted. A set of criteria has been agreed to measure outcomes and a research proposal is under consideration linked to the assessment of all clients.

The Commission has visited all the units since their formation, although not all were operational at the time, mainly due to delays in recruiting consultant psychiatrists, but also due to an intentionally staged process of admission. In general, the environments are suitable and offer privacy and space within the secure setting.

In the independent sector, the Commission visits four relatively large independent sector hospitals, which have significant medium secure facilities:

> Kneesworth House – 159 bed hospital in Hertfordshire
> Stockton Hall – a 106 bed hospital near York
> Llanarth Court – a 64 bed hospital in Gwent
> St Andrews – a 422 bed hospital in Northampton

The first three listed are managed by Partnerships in Care, which has also opened another 60-bedded unit, Redford Lodge in North London. The Commission made its first visit there in February 1996 and was impressed with the facilities and ethnic mix of the staffing. Its location is also readily accessible. These hospitals continue to make an important contribution to provision for patients with challenging behaviour.

The Commission takes a close interest in these hospitals because of their relatively large number of detained patients, which together accounted for about 300 admissions under the Mental Health Act in 1995/6. The Commission drew attention, in the Sixth Biennial Report (9.7), to its concerns about the lack of monitoring from the purchaser perspective. Places are purchased by a large number of authorities and there may be no one purchaser nominated to take the lead role in monitoring standards of care. This is the case at St. Andrew's and Stockton Hall. Kneesworth Hospital was without a lead purchaser until March 1996, when East London and City Health Authority assumed responsibility. Llanarth Court's lead purchaser is Bro Taff Health Authority. The Commission's new Guidance Note, *Guidance to Health Authorities*, should be of assistance to the lead purchaser in identifying priorities for monitoring compliance with the Act and Code of Practice.

4.4.2 Service Constraints

The expansion in medium secure hospital buildings has not been matched by an increase in other resources, particularly staffing and discharge facilities, which, in some regions, has acted as a brake on the full development of the service.

Staff shortages, examples of which are quoted in the previous section, have prevented several units from keeping open their full complement of beds.

Fromeside Clinic, RSU, Frenchay Healthcare NHS Trust: Visit 3.10.96

Commission members acknowledged that there were persistent problems with staff recruitment and that further bed closures and ECRs might be necessary. Four beds had already been closed, following a review of staff numbers, and there had been a rise in the number of violent attacks by patients. This reduction in beds was in addition to the non-commissioning of a further 4, which had left the unit short by a total of 8 beds. It is likely that admissions requiring this unit's level of security will be hindered, that excessive pressure will be created on the acute service and that patients awaiting discharge from high security provision will be affected.

Denis Hill Unit, RSU, Bethlem and Maudsley NHS Trust: Visit 12.2.96

Problems with the recruitment and retention of qualified nursing staff have been identified as one of the causal factors in blocking 4 of the 25 beds normally available for medium secure provision. The situation was further aggravated by the fact that few of the patients had made sufficient progress to enable their transfer to hostel accommodation, where one of the five places remained vacant.

These problems also have the effect of lowering staff morale, reducing the range of therapeutic services and daytime activity and constraining regimes so that they may become too rigid to allow for individualised attention to personal needs.

Ashen Hill, RSU, Eastbourne & County Healthcare NHS Trust: Visit 22/3.4.96

Commission members were pleased to see the extension of this building, but were concerned that staff were having to cope with an increase in the number of disturbed and unsettled patients. This situation seemed to have lasted for many months and the effect on staff morale was noticeable. Staff tended to work overtime to cover specialling, particularly in relation to disturbed patients. This had worked well in the past, when a similar situation lasted only a matter of weeks, but with the present situation having been going on for many months, the stress on staff should be reviewed. A very high use of seclusion was noted over the past two months. Commission members were also concerned to hear of the abnormal workload of the Responsible Medical Officer who was now covering both Ashen Hill and Southview. They were, however, pleased to hear that an appointment of an additional consultant has been made, which should ease the present burden of the consultant in post. Several of the patients detained within Ashen Hill complained of the lack of activity during the daytime. However, it is noted that, although there had been no occupational therapy for the past eight or nine months, the situation had improved dramatically recently, with two new appointments and a further one in the pipeline.

Kenneth Day Unit, Northgate and Prudhoe NHS Trust: Visit 14.11.96

Commission members were aware of patient discontent on Cheviot Ward, where they received complaints about the apparent lack of access to fresh air and exercise. They received comments which suggested the daily activity regimes were too restrictive, at the expense of meeting individual patient need. Despite this, the conclusion was reached that the unit provided a generally high standard of patient care and treatment planning.

Some units, more than others, have been able to create an environment with the requisite physical facilities and activity programme to provide an adequate quality of life and stimulation for patients who must reside with them for up to two years.

Wathwood Hospital, RSU, Rotherham Priority Care NHS Trust: Visit 19.2.97

Services were observed to be exemplary. En-suite rooms were the norm. The seclusion room, although it had not yet been used, was found to need attention. Minor changes to fittings were recommended to maximise patient safety. Otherwise, Commission members were very impressed, highlighting, in particular, the number of disturbed patients receiving very low doses of medication and the risk assessments undertaken on each ward round and then clearly filed at the front of case notes.

The problems of providing adequate standards of care while patients are in hospital are aggravated by difficulties in arranging for discharge, such as obtaining the necessary social work input and suitable 'move on' accommodation. Difficulties are also caused by failures of Health and Local Authorities to reach agreement over their respective funding responsibilities and by patchy implementation of the Care Programme Approach. It may be necessary for Regional Secure Units to take the initiative in securing suitable after-care arrangements.

Edenfield Unit, Mental Health Services of Salford NHS Trust: Visit 29.2.96

Local Social Workers expressed alarm at the rate of growth of the unit, which was producing more demands than they could meet. The discharge problems experienced by the unit were exacerbated by difficulties in gaining the co-operation of community-based care managers, in securing financial agreements with purchasing authorities and in providing the social work input required.

Crozier Terrace, RSU, City and Hackney Community Services NHS Trust: Visit 19.9.96

The unit had made concerted efforts towards achieving a more integrated care service. It has provided the funding for five Community Psychiatric Nurses within the locality teams, so as to provide for the high number of patients who were on the equivalent after-care level to a Supervision Register. The new resource was to be line managed by the Hospital, although a decision had not been reached as to the allocation of workloads.

4.4.3 Diversity of Need

The pressures on medium secure beds remain high, with many units operating waiting lists. Units are faced with competing demands from:

- patients waiting for transfer to conditions of lower security than their current placement;

- patients presenting difficult to manage / challenging behaviour, where local services are unable to cope;

- individuals in prison, who should be receiving treatment in a psychiatric setting.

These groups of patients have diverse needs, which are difficult to meet in a single setting. For example, the special needs and security risks presented by some prison transfers oblige changes to be made in the regime that are unhelpful to others. Patients' relatives and staff have expressed serious concerns at care being provided in proximity to patients with a criminal background.

Suggestions have been made to meet the situation by creating separate wards for prison transfers in each regional unit, or by developing dedicated regional units for them. In view of the considerable staff and user dissatisfaction with the present patient mix, the Commission would like to see the problem quantified, alternative solutions examined and the attention of purchasing authorities drawn to the issue.

Some medium secure units have developed a culture of not admitting or retaining difficult patients, so that, even when there is a vacancy, they may reject referrals when they regard an acute unit's professed inability to cope with a 'difficult to manage' patient insufficient justification for admission to a secure facility. Some units will accept patients detained on Section 3, but not on Section 2, although Section 3 may not always be appropriate, for instance for some disturbed individuals of uncertain diagnosis found wandering by the police.

There is a concern that local Trusts may lose confidence and skills in dealing with those severely mentally ill patients who are difficult to manage. Although local Trusts need to develop their own provision for patients with 'difficult to manage' behaviour, the Commission view is that Regional Secure Units should keep under review the total needs of their catchment area and be prepared to provide readily accessible advice and support in emergencies to local acute units.

Patient mix may be particularly problematic for women, especially where they have been victims of sexual abuse and find themselves sharing ward facilities with male patients, who may also have been sexual offenders. Several Visit Reports have identified a need for Medium Secure Units to address more effectively the issue of women's safety and privacy. Some have already responded to the challenge.

Arnold Lodge, RSU, Leicester Mental Health Services NHS Trust: Visit 27.2.97

The unannounced Visit was carried out to survey a number of issues, including the adequacy of the environment and services for women. Commission members were informed that female patients, who represented over a fifth of the patients at that time, were resident on three of the six mixed wards, but the unit did not have a policy to ensure the safety of women. On all the wards visited, each female patient did have a single en-suite room, but there was concern at the spyholes in the bedroom and most toilet doors, allowing unseen viewing into their private areas by male patients as well as staff. Labelling of shared facilities was unclear and there was no other space reserved for women only. Staff on Pennine Ward explained that the sole major incident of sexual harassment occurring over the last twelve months had been reported to police. The managers were confident that staff were sufficiently aware of the special needs of women's in a secure mental health setting and that training was provided.

Three Bridges, RSU, West London Healthcare NHS Trust: Visit 24.5.96

Women residents at the Three Bridges Unit were uncomfortable at being subjected to explicit conversations between fellow male patients and furthermore, at not being able to lock their doors. The Trust has actively responded to this concern by considering the provision of separate gender facilities in the 1997/8 planning programme

Caswell Clinic, Bridgend and District NHS Trust: Visit 14.11.96

The unannounced Visit revealed a largely commendable service for women, since they could be assured that a female staff member would be on duty at all times and separate sleeping accommodation, plus bathroom and toilet facilities were readily available. The wards were well-staffed and adequately covered the supervision of disturbed patients. Regular training on sexuality and related issues was provided. Physical restraint was seldom required and the standards of care continued to be of very high quality.

4.4.4 Contact with Home Area and After-Care Arrangements

There are varying policies about extra-contractual referrals (ECRs). Some units reserve beds for this purpose so as to attract additional funding; others, such as the Bracton Clinic, seek to avoid out-of district placements and allow all the beds to be used to meet local demand.

Medium Secure Units in the independent sector depend on funding from ECRs and sometimes struggle to meet the challenge of maintaining relationships with their patients' home areas.

There are inevitable difficulties in maintaining contact with family and planning for after-care when people are placed at a considerable distance from home. It is an important component in the therapeutic programme for most patients to have visits from family and a well-planned transfer back to the home area. However, relatives may be unable to afford to visit regularly. They are only entitled to claim travel expenses if they are receiving Income Support. The issue was raised with the Commission by the management at Kneesworth Hospital. The majority of their patients are referred from London Authorities, but there are no provisions for the referring Authorities to subsidise travelling costs for relatives.

Financial constraints also interfere with the attendance of social workers at Section 117 meetings. Lambeth Social Services, for example, said they could not afford to release a social worker on a day visit for such a meeting for patients placed by the Health Authority at a distant hospital. Local agencies may be reluctant to become involved when they have no appropriate accommodation and after-care services to offer. On the Commission Visit to St Andrew's in October 1996, one patient under Section 3 was reported to have been waiting for a transfer to Devon since July, but this had not taken place because of a lack of a firm commitment from the local Consultant to become the patient's RMO. The Commission will continue to impress on local purchasing authorities the importance of accepting their responsibilities in such circumstances.

The Commission have also emphasised the responsibilities of hospitals to implement Section 117 procedures.

St. Andrew's Hospital, Northampton: Visits May and Oct. 1996

It was noted during the Visit in May that one patient had had no Section 117 meeting either before or after being discharged the previous January. The Hospital responded by instigating an audit of Section 117. However, at the October Visit there were still problems about discharges.

There is evidence to suggest that where procedures are rigorously applied, outside agencies respond more positively. For example, the Commission has commended the standards of Section 117 after-care planning and recording at Kneesworth House since the introduction of a care co-ordinator for each patient and a more comprehensive policy for the Care Programme Approach. Attendance of local authority representatives at after-care meetings has improved since these measures were taken.

Other innovative solutions should be sought to improve after-care planning. The normal pattern is for professionals to be invited to Section 117 meetings at the hospital, as recommended in the Code of Practice (27.6). However, the proposed revisions to the Code envisage more flexibility. It has been suggested that specific reference to meetings being held in hospital should be removed. One solution may be for the meetings to take place at a more convenient location for the local agencies. For example, the RMO and a team nurse from Smythe Ward, St Andrew's, have sometimes accompanied a patient to a care planning meeting in the home area. Another idea which has been proposed is the use of telephone conferencing for Section 117 meetings.

The Commission has also drawn the attention of the Mental Nursing Homes to the need to hold Section 117 meetings before a Tribunal hearing. This recommendation has been reinforced in the proposed revisions of the Code of Practice, which states that a discussion of after-care needs (with Social Services participation) should take place before a patient has a Tribunal or Managers' hearing, so that suitable after-care arrangements can be implemented in the event of a discharge. Patients are, in fact, occasionally discharged contrary to the recommendations of the RMO and it is important to be prepared for such an outcome.

The Commission will continue to urge that effective after-care planning takes place, including planning prior to any Tribunal hearing. It recognises the logistical difficulties in convening multi-agency meetings and that a large number of applications are made by patients in the Medium Secure Hospitals. But there is the overriding concern that those placed far from home should not be at greater risk of being discharged without adequate local service arrangements being made or should not be obliged to remain in hospital for longer than necessary.

4.5   High Security Hospital Issues

4.5.1 A Distinctive Service

The High Security Psychiatric Hospitals (**Ashworth, Broadmoor** and **Rampton**) receive patients assessed as potentially dangerous and who require treatment for mental disorder. Most are detained under Part III of the Act as a consequence of criminal proceedings but approximately one fifth are subject to civil detention.

Patients in high secure care generally stay for much longer periods than other detained patients (the average being 7 to 8 years) and are subject to stringent legal conditions. For these reasons the Commission has always attached great importance to the pursuit of its statutory responsibilities at the three hospitals, in particular by meeting and interviewing detained patients, in private, and inquiring into matters they draw to the attention of Commission members. The Commission has a responsibility to monitor the use of the Mental Health Act and Code of Practice and to administer the

'Consent to Treatment' provisions of the Act, but it is not an inspectorate concerned with the monitoring of standards generally. However, it does devote part of its time at the High Security Hospitals to examining systematically a small number of matters directly related to the care, treatment and quality of life of patients detained in the three hospitals; for example, the adequacy of seclusion rooms at **Ashworth Hospital**, the implementation of the Care Programme Approach (CPA) at **Broadmoor Hospital** and the provision of patient activities at **Rampton Hospital**.

In 1994, the European Committee for the Prevention of Torture and Inhuman or Degrading Treatment or Punishment (C.P.T.), as part of one of its routine visits to the United Kingdom, visited Rampton Hospital. Its report together with the response of the U.K. Government was published in March 1996 (Council of Europe, 1996). The report referred to a wide range of issues including full implementation of the Code of Practice guidance on the handling of aggression, the need to improve doctor : patient ratio and night staffing levels and the urgent need to ensure that all patients have, at least, one hour outdoor exercise per day. Many of the report's findings replicate those of the Commission. The implementation of the Committee's recommendations is being monitored at Rampton Hospital.

The goal of delivering consistently high standards of care, while taking adequately into account the legitimate interests of patients, staff and the wider public, continues to prove difficult to achieve in the High Security Hospitals, notwithstanding the progress made in recent years and the examples of good practice that can be found in each.

The task is not made easier by the hospitals' controversial and difficult past or their high and, usually negative, public profile. The most recent examples are the widespread media coverage given, at the beginning of 1997, to allegations about criminal activities on a unit at Ashworth (which led to the establishment of an Inquiry under Judge Peter Fallon) and allegations about security and the "power" of patients at Broadmoor (which led to an external management review of patient care and security).

On 31st March 1996 the Special Health Services Authority (SHSA) ceased to exist and the High Security Psychiatric Services Commissioning Board was established with responsibility for, among other things, commissioning services from the three High Security Hospitals. The hospitals themselves became individual Special Health Authorities in their own right, responsible for managing the High Security Hospitals as separate provider units in much the same way that other NHS hospitals are managed by NHS Trusts. Each relates to their local NHS Executive Regional Office. During this period of organisational and structural change the Commission has formed links and established reporting arrangements with all these bodies, which together are responsible for the management, commissioning and monitoring of high security services.

During the period under review, the Commission identified a number of issues for special attention, which are described below.

4.5.2 Care Planning, Treatment and the Provision of Therapy

The three High Security Hospitals are the only providers of high security care in England and Wales and are therefore specialist facilities which should offer correspondingly specialist treatment of the highest quality for a particularly challenging group of patients.

The basis of such provision should be competent treatment planning, examples of which can be found in all three hospitals. The Commission is concerned, however, that too often treatment planning is inadequate and too frequently it hardly extends beyond medication and containment. Across all three hospitals there is patchy and generally insufficient participation by disciplines other than doctors and nurses. The detail and frequency of reviews of treatment plans and nursing care plans should correspond to the complexity of the patient's background, problems, rehabilitation needs and changes in their mental state. Too often this does not occur. A major contributor to these difficulties, especially at Broadmoor and Rampton is the shortage of various disciplines (see below), notably psychologists. The individual case loads of Responsible Medical Officers (RMOs) in the three hospitals are significantly higher than in the Regional Secure Units and at Rampton the number of unfilled consultant vacancies during the period under review has significantly impaired the hospital's pursuit of its therapeutic objectives. The shortage of various disciplines is not however the only significant reason for the patchy quality of treatment planning in the hospitals. A major challenge for those responsible for the commissioning and provision of high secure care is the successful establishment of standards of treatment and care planning that is genuinely multi-disciplinary. The challenge they face is evidenced by the Commission's experience of the implementation of the Care Programme Approach (CPA) and Section 117 after-care, which can best be described as variable throughout the three hospitals.

The Care Programme Approach

At **Broadmoor**, RMOs have shown limited enthusiasm in applying the hospital's policy, nurses have found the paperwork burdensome, forms in hospital notes have been absent or largely uncompleted and much activity has remained unrecorded. Social workers have been active in after-care, but have kept separate records. A Targeted Commission Visit found variable practice, lack of standardisation of documentation, insufficient needs assessments, inadequate involvement of responsible local authorities and limited planning for Tribunal discharges. The Medical Director is to chair a new strategy group to promote the CPA. At **Ashworth**, Commission members have been disappointed at the slow progress in developing the CPA and doubt that the hospital will meet its own targets. Operating the system makes major demands on manpower and there is an urgent need for CPA training for staff in all disciplines. At **Rampton** a training programme for ward managers and a procedural manual has been introduced. While patient records show evidence of CPA planning and multi-disciplinary meetings taking place for patients about to leave hospital, it was observed that some patients had several concurrent care plans; a separate care plan for each problem they present, which negates the main purpose of the CPA. Some staff misguidedly thought that CPA / Section 117 is unnecessary for patients moving to medium secure facilities rather than the community.

A prerequisite for the provision of coherent and coordinated care is a record system which makes explicit what each patient's needs are, how they will be met, who is responsible for carrying out each action and who the keyworker is. Where there are needs which cannot be met within the current level and type of provision, these should be documented and fed back into the planning process. More must also be done to engage responsible health and local authorities throughout a patient's periods of stay at the High Security Hospitals. This will facilitate effective and timely preparation for transfers to less secure care and encourage authorities to ensure that the facilities required may be made available.

Consent to Treatment

Central to the Commission's activities in the High Security Hospitals is its monitoring of the implementation of the Consent to Treatment safeguards set out in Part IV of the Act. Shortcomings in the completion by RMOs of Form 38, certifying the patient's consent, are still too frequent at all three High Security Hospitals.

At **Broadmoor** forms are not always signed by the current RMO, especially following changes of ward or consultant. Some drugs given to patients are not covered by Form 38; Commission members have often reminded nurses of their professional responsibility to ensure that all drugs they administer are given legally. In contravention of Commission advice, superseded statutory forms still appear uncancelled together with the current form. Form MHAC1, used for reporting to the Commission reviews of treatment in statutorily defined circumstances has not been completed by some RMOs and the Code's guidance about giving the patient a copy has not been followed. At **Rampton**, Commission members have noted that the frequent changes of RMO and dependence on locum consultants have produced doubts about the validity of some certificates of patient's consent. However, where this has been pointed out by the Commission and a subsequent review by a Second Opinion Appointed Doctor has taken place, the treatment given has, in most cases, been certified appropriate. At **Ashworth,** one RMO consistently fails to conform to the Code's advice about Form 38. But Commission members have noticed an improvement in the quality of the Forms completed by other RMOs. They have been assisted in this by the attendance of the pharmacist on the wards. There are significant differences between the three Hospitals in the frequency of requests to the Commission for Second Opinions under Section 58 of the Act. The reasons for this are to be examined.

Staffing

The deployment and adequacy of staff is only a matter for the Commission where deficiencies appear to impact directly on the care and treatment of patients. During the period under review, the Commission has noted difficulties at both Broadmoor and Rampton.

At **Broadmoor** there were, at one time, 50 nurse vacancies and the numbers actually on duty in some wards appeared sometimes to have been reduced to unacceptable levels; for instance when only two staff were on night duty in one of the male intensive care wards. Managers have had to telephone around the hospital to find staff and nurses often do not know the patients on the wards to which they are assigned. There has been high turnover of RMOs with some wards having at least 9 changes over a period of about 4 or 5 years. There have also been shortages and many changes of psychologists and social workers within clinical teams.

At **Rampton,** the staff situation has led to numerous changes in the composition of nursing shifts, with patients complaining of not knowing the identity of their 'named nurse' or long periods when it is not possible to speak to him or her. The continuing serious difficulty in recruiting consultant psychiatrists because of retirement or leaving to take up new appointments has exacerbated an already unsatisfactory situation, causing anxiety for patients, disruption of treatment plans and delays in reports to Tribunals.

At **Ashworth,** there is not the same shortage of medical staff, but problems are encountered in recruiting sufficient nursing staff, particularly on the female wards. Bank staff and nurses from other wards are frequently used, resulting in a loss of continuity of care. Commission members have also noted the replacement of qualified nurses by less qualified staff, whose relative lack of experience and expertise can sometimes be detrimental to effective patient care. A shortage of clinical psychologists has limited the provision of psychological therapies, again particularly for women patients.

Patient Mix

The hospitals care for a group of patients with a wide range of needs. On occasion the Commission has observed that patients with different needs are placed in the same wards to their mutual detriment.

At **Broadmoor**, which has experienced high occupancy and a waiting list for a long time, patients are sometimes moved to make space rather than for clinical reasons and are placed on wards unable to meet their needs. The pre-discharge wards, for example, house some patients who are still highly dependent. However, there have been improvements to the intensive care wards, which have been divided to provide small separate intensive care groups.

At **Rampton**, there have been a number of concerns including :

- the mix of women with learning disability with those with mental illness;

- the management of a large (17 – 20) group of women with behavioural difficulties on a confined ward;

- the exploitation of vulnerable patients by patients with psychopathic disorder on an admission ward.

The proportion of patients with learning disabilities, which used to be large at Rampton, has been greatly reduced, following a successful programme of transfers of patients to accommodation in their area of origin. Those that remain have diverse needs and many present challenging behaviour. They are becoming difficult to care for effectively within the accommodation available, which was constructed for large groups of patients and offers inadequate protection for this vulnerable minority from harm and exploitation by other patients.

There needs to be careful consideration given to how to cater for diverse needs. The creation of specialist wards for particular groups of patients can also lead to difficulties. At **Ashworth**, patients are housed on wards according to their diagnosis. The placement of all patients with psychopathic disorder in one unit has caused management and security problems.

Patient Activities

The provision of purposeful activity is a fundamental element in an individual care programme, providing structure to everyday life and offering opportunity for social and psychological fulfilment. However, securing the participation of patients who are liable to spend many years in an institution, where motivation may be lacking and staffing stretched, is not an easy task.

The level of activity of a sample of patients at **Broadmoor** was measured during a Targeted Visit in mid-1996. It was found that in a group of 25 patients from 8 wards, none were provided with more than 25 hours of structured activity per week off the ward (the standard established by the SHSA) and 10 had less than 6 hours. Among a sub-sample of 13 patients, 10 had less than 2 hours structured activity on the ward. There are also problems with less structured activity and social events. Broadmoor lacks indoor sports facilities and an indoor swimming pool, which the other hospitals find very beneficial. The exercise equipment on some wards has not been used because staff have not had the necessary training in supervision. Patients have expressed frustration when social events have been cancelled, sometimes at extremely short notice, depriving them of their principal opportunity to meet patients from other wards and to communicate with patients of the opposite sex. At **Ashworth**, the rehabilitation facilities are of a high standard, but are underused by patients, who tend to spend large parts of the day in their side-rooms. Patients at all the hospitals have also commented on the restricted availability of on-ward and off-ward activities, especially during weekends and holiday periods. Shortage of staff is the usual reason given. Patient outings have also suffered a substantial drop apparently because of a reduction in funding for overtime.

Access to fresh air has been a long-standing concern for the Commission and, in the last Biennial Report, was highlighted as a matter which must be given the highest priority over the following two years. The minimum quality standard, which was set by the Special Health Services Authority, is 10 hours access to fresh air per patient per week in the Summer and four hours per week in Winter. At **Rampton**, there has been encouraging progress towards the achievement of an agreed standard. However, some areas lag behind and need managerial encouragement. Major building works and refurbishment, together with changes of nursing staff, have interfered with the fresh air policy. At **Broadmoor**, records indicate that on some wards there has been minimal access to fresh air. On the female intensive care ward, for example, during one week in summer (1996), the maximum access for any patient was 3 hours 10 minutes; most patients having significantly less than this. During October 1996, no access to fresh air was recorded for patients on Sheffield ward. The monitoring of access to fresh air has varied in thoroughness and some records may understate provision made, but it is clear that many patients receive nowhere near adequate opportunities for fresh air. There is a need for staff in the three High Security Hospitals to pursue standards more vigorously and for systematic monitoring to continue, especially in relation to those patients unable to go out unless supervised.

4.5.3 Control and Discipline (see also 10.2)

Finding the balance between maintaining discipline within the institution and the preservation of the therapeutic goal of personal responsibility is particularly difficult in the High Security Hospitals. The tightening of security measures in order to control the behaviour of some patients may seem unduly restrictive for others. For example, the recent allegations about the acquisition of pornographic videos by patients at Ashworth Hospital have led to the imposition of greater restrictions on the use of personal videos and computers in all the High Security Hospitals.

Measures of security to ensure safety and the efficient running of the institution are most clearly needed against activities which are dangerous or criminal. If such behaviours are not reported and dealt with as crimes, there must be some clear alternative means of responding to them. An example is the possession of, using and trading in illicit drugs. There is a growing awareness of this problem in the High Security Hospitals, in part, possibly associated with an influx of patients from prisons, which have their own well-documented, institutional drug cultures. The Commission has long identified this as a particular problem at Ashworth Hospital and it conducted a review of suspected drug use between February and March 1997. Staff were interviewed and ward records examined. The review team found that staff on the mental illness wards on the North site had suspicions that just over one quarter of the patients might have used drugs illicitly, but there was very little information available about possible drug use on the Personality Disorder Unit and other wards on the East site. The Commission has recommended that Ashworth Hospital introduce more proactive security and control measures.

Restrictive measures must be reasonable and clearly tied to the purpose for which they were imposed. For example, incoming mail can be withheld if it is thought necessary to do so in the interests of the safety of the patient or for the protection of others, but not for any other reason.

A Broadmoor patient's complaint about the withholding of mail led to the discovery that patients' mail from the Benefits Agency and other mail relating to finances was routinely intercepted. The Medical Records Department dealt with Benefits mail, helping to complete forms and ensuring return to the Department of Social Security. However, patients were not informed when such mail did not reach them. The Director of Patient Care has agreed that this practice is outside the provisions of the Act concerning the withholding of mail (Section 134) and that it will be discontinued.

The Commission does, in fact, have a statutory duty under Section 121(7) of the Act to review decisions by the Managers of the High Security Hospitals to withhold postal packets. Such decisions are reviewed by the Commission at the request of the patient and the Commission is entitled to order the release of the postal packet. During this reporting period, there were nine such requests. On two occasions, the Commission ordered the release of the mail (including the above example), on five occasions the

Commission upheld the decisions of the Managers and the other two cases are still being investigated.

Seclusion (see 10.1)

The use of seclusion requires close scrutiny and members pay special attention to its implementation on their Visits to each of the hospitals. Any concerns about its use in individual cases are immediately drawn to the attention of the relevant authorities. At the beginning of 1997, the Commission were particularly concerned about a specific incident at Ashworth Hospital where a patient died following a week in seclusion and drew the matter to the attention of the Secretary of State. The outcome of the inquest and a hospital inquiry are awaited.

Commission members have observed that practice does not always accord with the hospital's own policy on seclusion. At **Ashworth** Hospital a new seclusion policy, broadly in accord with the Code of Practice, was being implemented in 1996. The Commission conducted a comprehensive review and found that there was considerable variation in the manner in which seclusion was undertaken and documented. The initial decision to seclude a patient and the reasons for it — commonly an actual or potential threat to staff or other patients — were being properly recorded. However, subsequent actions, the periodic reviews and medical approval for the continuation of seclusion were not entered on many record forms. There was a concentration of more disturbed patients on a few wards, where 3 or 4 seclusions would occur each day, some lasting several days. This put pressure on the staff and lowered the standard of record keeping. It was recommended that the various recording practices should be reviewed and the good practices on some wards introduced on others, aided by a programme of training for staff. At **Rampton** Hospital the Commission raised with managers similar concerns about compliance with the hospital's seclusion policy, such as the recording and review of each episode of seclusion and its consequences. On one of the women's wards, patients commented on the way in which seclusion was followed by a period of close observation, which they interpreted as punishment. Managers were persuaded that seclusion procedures were in need of review and agreed to consider all the points raised by the Commission.

At **Broadmoor** Hospital some wards no longer use seclusion, but on others, mainly the intensive care wards, it remains common. Frequent usage may indicate insufficient consideration of alternative approaches, such as 'talking down' aggressive patients or preventively providing constructive activity and exercise. It should never be used to reduce the risk that the patient may take his own life or harm himself (Code of Practice, 18.15); yet "own safety" and "self harm" have been recorded as reasons for resort to seclusion.

There were also occasional failures at Broadmoor to meet the hospital's self-imposed standard for the doctor to attend within one hour of the application of seclusion; (the Code of Practice states that a doctor should "attend immediately"). Given the frequency of patient disturbance on intensive care wards, doctors have sometimes displayed casual attitudes, such as stopping to attend to other matters while on route to a seclusion incident. Reviews are not normally carried out during the night; the first morning review has sometimes occurred after 11.00 a.m. Independent reviews by a team not directly involved with the patient's treatment are not carried out according to the Code of Practice (18.20). Commission members have also been critical of loosely filed seclusion records; the hospital has since agreed to the Commission's recommendation of using bound books.

Broadmoor Hospital operates two distinctive practices in addition to routine seclusion. For patients who present a persistent risk to other patients and staff and who cannot be controlled otherwise, seclusion may be extended over a lengthy period during which patients may spend significant periods out of seclusion, but can be returned without staff completing the usual documentation. These cases are notified to senior managers who become involved in reviewing them. The second practice, known as 'segregation', consists of refusal of access to other patients except when specifically permitted. This occurs where a patient is thought liable to be dangerous and unpredictably violent. The regime may continue for a long time. The Commission has advised that such patients should always have access to staff, be able to see visitors under suitable conditions, be told of their right to contact a legal advisor and the Commission and that independent and qualified clinicians participate in reviews.

It is also important to ensure that the conditions in which patients are secluded are adequate. The Commission conducted an unannounced inspection of the seclusion rooms at Ashworth Hospital and found that whilst nearly all were clean and well ventilated, none were perfectly adapted to their purpose. Sharp edges, dimmer lights not working, hazardous wooden bed frames, windows shuttered and obscuring all natural light, unsuitable carpeted floors, inadequately shielded radiators, observational 'blind spots' and an absence of call systems or privacy flaps on observation panels were noted. A number of the rooms were considered unsafe and, in the Commission's view need urgent attention. All these matters have been taken up with the hospital.

Restraint (see 10.2.3)

The Commission was concerned about an incident at Broadmoor Hospital in 1996 when a team of nurses in protective clothing, using a shield with projecting bolts, entered a seclusion room to disarm a patient of a broken cup which he was brandishing with threats against staff. Commission members agreed with the Director of Patient Care that there was a need for adequate policy guidelines for such circumstances, which should include obtaining authorization from senior clinical staff, immediate medical examination of the patient where injuries may have occurred and a subsequent review and debriefing of the staff involved.

There is also concern about the use of protective clothing to restrain patients, which is hardly ever seen except in the High Security Hospitals, but is commonly used in the intensive care wards at Broadmoor. Secure clothing is used more frequently for women than men and there have been particular concerns about the loss of dignity suffered by a woman where her clothing is removed in the presence of a number of staff.

Training in methods of control and restraint is essential. At Ashworth, despite the development of a 'Care and Responsibility' course which is available for all staff and outside agencies, there is low take-up of places from within the hospital, which Commissioners are told, is often due to staffing problems.

There is a general need for clear, written policies dealing with aspects of control and discipline and more openness about them for patients. Many policies are out-of-date or have been left in uncompleted draft form or are not implemented, leading to inconsistency and confusion. Uniformity of approach is important. Patients may be disciplined for matters on which no official policy exists or on policies they have not heard about. Comments from the Commission are also better informed and more helpful when there are agreed standards and policies on which to base them.

4.5.4 Issues of Special Concern

The Care and Treatment of Women Patients

Women patients make up approximately 15% of the High Security Hospital patient population. Notwithstanding the determined efforts of many members of staff, it has to be concluded that the special needs of women patients, associated with self-harm, eating disorders, obesity, self care and sexuality, attract insufficient therapeutic endeavour in the predominantly male culture of the High Security Hospitals. Women appear disadvantaged relative to men in having less access to structured activity, social functions, recreation and parole opportunities. They are also more likely to be made the subject of restraint (see above) and seclusion. The seclusion returns at Broadmoor, for the last quarter of 1996, showed that 28% of women patients compared to 10% of men were secluded. At **Broadmoor**, the Women's Unit has had particular difficulties in recruiting staff and the high proportion of male staff on some shifts is unsatisfactory. Insensitivity on the part of some staff, who refer to patients as "girls" or make unsympathetic remarks about self harm, has also been noted. At **Rampton**, issues affecting the care of women have long been a topic of concern to the Commission. The range of recreational activity for women is poor in comparison to that provided for men. The regime on the admission ward is regarded as oppressive. Post-admission assessments for women and the approach to self harm are considered unsatisfactory, despite a clearly defined and operated policy of observation. A comprehensive proposal for the improvement of services for women is being considered by the Rampton Hospital Authority and following a review by the Commission of the present services undertaken early in 1997, the Commission continue to press for service improvements. At **Ashworth**, there are anxieties about rapid and unsettling changes in the management structure and staffing on two of the female wards, which have occurred during 1996/7. A lack of firm policy as to the role and function of the wards, a high sickness rate and numerous changes of staff have led to low morale among staff, which in turn has affected the care of patients and made the ward, at times, potentially unsafe. There is also a need for care and rehabilitation systems to focus more on women's needs and for an expansion of women-only facilities. A new Relationships Policy (see 10.2.4) is being introduced, but meanwhile women have felt unduly restricted. Following an alleged incident of rape, a total ban was imposed on communications between patients from male and female wards. This has now been relaxed to some extent, but the Commission would like to see more opportunities for socialisation.

Race and Culture

Race and culture remains a matter of particular concern at the High Security Hospitals. Adverse comments have been made about the standard of ethnic food, apparent unconcern on the part of staff at racist remarks by patients and the inadequate representation of ethnic minorities among staff. It may also be necessary to review cultural and religious preferences periodically, as some patients, who may appear disinterested initially, may change during their period of stay in hospital.

At **Rampton** the Commission continues to note a lack of awareness of racial issues amongst staff. It is accepted that there are individual attempts to deal with the issues, but the overall impression is of poor understanding of, and an uncoordinated approach to, differing cultural needs.

> At one Visit Commission members drew attention to a poster on a staff notice board that was defaced in a manner pointing to a gross lack of awareness of racial sensitivities on the part of staff on the ward in question.

Hospital managers at Rampton have been advised of the urgent need for staff training and policy guidance on racial issues to improve staff awareness and for practice to be monitored against agreed principles and regularly reviewed to ensure a viable and consistent approach.

At **Broadmoor,** ethnicity is commonly not recorded in the clinical notes; either there is no space on the front sheet or it is left blank. This raises a question about the process of identifying this information for monitoring purposes and whether it is based, as it should be, on the patient's own perception of their ethnicity. There have been occasions where patients have asked for the provision of psychotherapy from a therapist from the same ethnic background, but this has not been forthcoming because of the lack of availability of appropriate staff or additional funding.

At **Ashworth** Hospital a Transcultural Committee has been in existence since 1989. It has formulated a strategy, accepted by the hospital management in May 1996, which sets out key principles and the core services needed to fulfil them. Successful implementation of the strategy would require a plan of action with realistic targets and effective monitoring.

Advocacy

Advocacy is especially important for patients subject to severe and prolonged curtailment of liberty. An active advocacy service is in operation at **Rampton** with the Patients' Council meeting on a weekly basis. At **Ashworth**, the advocacy service continues to provide a comprehensive service to patients as well as support to the Patients' Council. At **Broadmoor** the Commissioning Board has only recently agreed initial funding to review the need for an advocacy service, although the hospital has had a Patients' Council for a number of years. The Commission is disappointed at the slow progress in establishing such a service. The Patients' Council was suspended for two weeks prior to the recent setting up of an external management review of patient care and security. This deprived patients of a channel to express views at a time when they were likely to be experiencing frustrations at some of the security measures being introduced. Allegations had been made that the Patients' Council within Broadmoor was unduly influencing the management of the hospital. The review team found no evidence to support this.

Transfer Delays

During a six month period from March through August 1996, Commissioners, helped by the staff at Ashworth Hospital, inquired into the reasons for delay in securing transfer of patients. Transfers to prisons and between wards within the hospital did not appear to involve undue waiting, but there were inordinate delays at every step in arrangements for transfers elsewhere. The Ashworth transfer list of April 1996 showed that, of 167 (37% of the patient population) patients officially listed as being in the process of transfer out, 31 had got to the stage where all parties involved had reached agreement. However, of these 31, 11 had been waiting over a year for implementation. Following agreement to proceed, some patients could wait for over two years to move out of the hospital. Those sent to another unit on Section 17 leave had a further substantial period waiting for their trial leave to be converted into a formal transfer.

There were 75 patients waiting either for funding by purchasers or for purchasers to find the provider unit to receive them. Of these, 18 had been waiting over a year. A further 61 were awaiting assessment by or reports from their prospective providers, or were waiting for Home Office agreement or for actual admission following a provider's favourable report.

Many delays were beyond the hospital's control. Purchasers were not funding sufficient places to meet the criteria for transfer within 6 months of agreement being reached, as set out in Department of Health Guidance (1994). Purchasers did not appear to be monitoring delays in providers producing the places they had promised who were also not committing themselves to firm dates, either for assessments or admissions. Some Regional Secure Units had daunting waiting lists, even when they had beds reserved for High Security Hospital transfers. Additional frustration and anti-therapeutic stress were being caused for patients by lack of communication to them of what stage their transfer processes had reached and worried patients often ask about this during Commission Visits.

4.5.5 A Need for Change

The establishment of another independent inquiry at Ashworth (The Fallon Inquiry), at the beginning of 1997, was singularly depressing, especially in light of the enormous endeavours in recent years to achieve real change in the three hospitals. Whatever the truth of the allegations the Inquiry will investigate, it is important to recognise the opportunity it presents to all those with a responsibility at Ashworth (including the Commission) to examine their own performance and contribute to the making of recommendations.

Its establishment also emphasises the urgent need for a coherent and long-term strategy for the future development of all types of secure care and the overwhelming importance of changing the way in which high secure care is delivered, so that it is capable of continuous improvement and able to reconcile the tensions between the need for safety within the institution and for the wider public and the patients' therapeutic needs and individual entitlements. Only then will the service be able to develop without the debilitating impact of periodic external inquiries and public criticism.

Chapter 5

Treatment and Consent

Summary

There were 10,216 referrals for statutory Second Opinions under the provisions of Section 58 in the reporting period, an increase of 8% over the previous period. Second Opinion referrals of women are more often for ECT; referrals of men more often for medication. A relatively high proportion of patients from Black ethnic groups are referred for medication.

While some units have made effective efforts to comply with the consent to treatment procedures of Section 58, deficiencies are too often apparent and on occasion the medication actually being given is not the same as certified on the statutory forms. The Commission will continue to point out errors, to remind doctors and nurses of their responsibilities in this regard and to recommend periodic audits.

Commission members often have doubts about the reality of a patient's understanding and consent. Assessment and recording of consent status should not be a mere paper exercise. The Commission strongly advises RMOs to record in case notes the interviews upon which they base their certification of a patient's consent on the statutory Form 38.

The obligation to provide a report under Section 61 (providing information on progress of treatment) is, at times, overlooked. The requirement to provide a copy of the Section 61 report to the patient is widely disregarded and should be implemented.

As a result of Second Opinion Appointed Doctor (SOAD) Visits, 15% of proposed treatment plans are modified.

Because SOAD Visits must sometimes be made out of working hours, units should make use of the notification of a visit to ensure that personnel are available to meet the requirement to consult a second professional.

Commission members continue to report that emergency treatment has been given to patients detained under the short sections of the Act or even to informal patients, which is outside the provisions of Section 62. The Commission is producing a Guidance Note on the use of Section 62, including a model form.

Recent legal cases have widened the definition of medical treatments for mental disorder without consent under Section 63 and the Commission is producing a Guidance Note. The detention and artificial feeding of patients with anorexia nervosa raises particular issues which the Commission has also addressed in a Guidance Note.

Referrals to the Panel for authorization of neurosurgery for mental disorder under the provisions of Section 57 remain few. Full compliance with Section 57 is especially difficult when referrals come from overseas. The Commission endorses proposals for standardised protocols and the systematic audit of neuro-surgery for mental disorder.

5 Treatment and Consent

5.1 Introduction

Aside from its general remit concerning the treatment and care of detained patients, the Commission has a duty under Section 121(a) of the Act to appoint medical practitioners to consider treatment plans for treatments falling within the provisions of Section 58, and also to appoint other persons as well as medical practitioners to validate treatments falling within the provisions of Section 57. This work, especially the organisation of Second Opinions for Section 58 treatments, makes heavy demands on the Commission's staff and takes up approximately one quarter of its budget.

Whilst the decisions made by Section 57 and 58 appointees are their responsibility alone, the basic procedures that have to be followed to reach them, as well as the forms on which validations are recorded, are set out in the Mental Health Act and its Regulations. The Commission not only monitors implementation, but offers guidance and advice to its appointees. This is overseen by the Commission's Consent to Treatment Group, which is a Special Interest Group of Commission members with relevant experience. It is responsible to the Commission Management Board for the operation of the Commission's duties under Part IV of the Act.

The Commission has produced leaflets for patients (see 3.1.3) on Consent to Treatment which are designed to be readable and easily understood without oversimplifying the law. The Commission would welcome comments on their availability and usefulness.

5.2 Treatments Requiring Consent or a Second Opinion

Section 58 defines conditions where certification by a medical practitioner appointed by the Commission is required before detained patients can be given specific treatments in the absence of consent. These treatments are currently medicine for mental disorder after the first three months of treatment in any continuous period of detention under the Act and electro-convulsive therapy (ECT) at any time. For these treatments to be given either the Responsible Medical Officer (RMO) must certify (on Form 38) that the patient has the capacity to consent and does so, or a Commission-appointed doctor (known as a Second Opinion Appointed Doctor or SOAD) must authorize the treatment on Form 39.

There were 10,216 referrals for a second opinion between July 1995 and April 1997, as is shown below according to the Mental Health Act categories of mental disorder:

Mental Health Act Category	No.
Mental Illness	9371
Mental Impairment	213
Severe Mental Impairment	113
Psychopathic Disorder	116
Dual Diagnosis	403
Total	10216

This represents an increase of about 8%, pro rata, over the previous reporting period. The increase may in part be a reflection of the increase in the number of patients detained under the Act during this period, but a greater awareness of consent issues (for example, when there is doubt about a patient's capacity or willingness to maintain their consent — see 5.2.1) may have also contributed. Three fifths of these referrals were for medication and just over a third for ECT; a small proportion were for treatment plans involving both medication and ECT. There were significant variations, according to the gender and ethnicity of patients, in the types and frequency of treatments for which referrals were made. Men and women were referred in roughly equal numbers, but men more often for medication and women more often for ECT.

Figure 8: Second opinions – gender/treatment

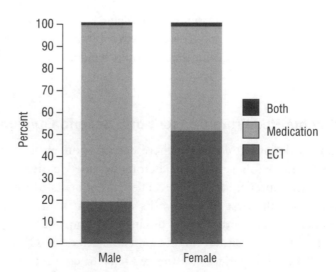

Of all referrals, 82.5% were for White patients, 12% for Black and 5.5% for Asian and other ethnic groups combined. There was a difference in the pattern of referral between ethnic groups (as can be seen in the chart below) with a higher proportion of patients from Black ethnic groups being referred for medication. This is likely to be reflection of the gender balance, as over 70% of Black patients referred for a Second Opinion were male.

Figure 9: Second opinions – ethnicity/treatment

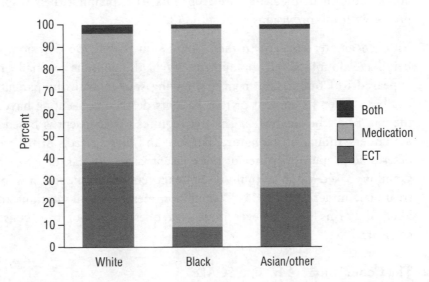

A new computerised system to record details of Second Opinion referrals was introduced in November, 1996. This will enable the Commission to refine the analysis of the data in its future Reports.

5.2.1. The Authenticity of Consent

Consent certificates (Forms 38) are regularly examined on Commission Visits and the treatment actually being given is compared to the treatment recorded on the certificates. Some units have effective monitoring of compliance and overall there has been an improvement, but many Visit Reports still cite examples of failure to comply with guidance in the Code of Practice on the completion of Forms 38, such as:

- Forms not completed by the patient's current RMO

- changed treatment plans not covered by Form 38

- details of Form 38 incomplete

- 'as required' (PRN) medication not included on Form 38

Commission members have also noted that clinical notes often contain no record of a discussion with patients about the proposed treatment around the time that the Form 38, certifying that they have understood and consented to such treatment, is signed by the RMO. Sometimes Forms 38 are not kept with the prescription cards and are therefore not immediately available for nurses to check that the agreed treatment plan is being adhered to at the time that they are administering the treatment. Generally, nursing staff appear unfamiliar with the Commission's Practice Note No.2 on the administration of medicine (see Appendix 4) explaining their responsibilities in complying with the provisions of Section 58.

An even greater concern to the Commission is that, on occasion, Commission members have doubts about the authenticity of the consent certified on Forms 38. It has appeared to Commission members, having spoken with the patients, that compliance has been taken as consent or that patients deemed consenting have little awareness of the nature of the treatment. The Act requires that consent is based upon an appropriate understanding of the nature, purpose and likely effects of the treatment. Failure to determine properly whether or not consent is present can deprive patients of a Second Opinion based upon a multi-disciplinary consultation and a subsequent review of treatment under Section 61. Commission members will continue to question the validity of Forms 38 whenever there is a question about true consent or capacity to consent.

5.2.2 The Commission's Advice to SOADs

The Commission's Consent to Treatment Group arranges training for SOADs and also provides guidance. SOADs are advised, for instance, that medicinal treatment authorized on Forms 39 should not normally be described by named preparations, but by the British National Formulary category to which such preparations belong, indicating the number of preparations authorised from that category and their upper dose limit. This advice is slightly more specific than that found in the current Code of Practice on the completion of Forms 38 (16.12). It allows SOADs to set a clear ceiling on what is authorized, while leaving sufficient leeway for the RMO to tailor the treatment to the precise needs of the patient in that slight changes can be made to the treatment without a further Second Opinion being arranged.

There are certain clinical circumstances when it is advisable to authorize a named drug preparation. The Commission does, for example, request SOADs to specify the inclusion or exclusion of clozaril from their authorizations on Forms 39. In this reporting period a number of new, recently licenced, anti-psychotic preparations have been prescribed for the treatment of some detained patients who had not responded to established treatments. These drugs became available before their appearance in the BNF. In these circumstances, SOADs and RMOs have to take note that the usual description of drugs by BNF category and dose range used on Consent forms has to be modified; the individual name of the drug and a specific dose range must be recorded. It is necessary that these new drugs are specifically and accurately referred to in the statutory documentation. Their effects in combination with other drugs are not always established (see 5.2.4) and it is important for the RMO and SOAD to be able to demonstrate that this has been taken into account.

The Consent to Treatment Group has been in discussion with SOADs over the issue of the authorization of 'as required' (PRN) medication. It is easy for such occasionally used treatments to result in a higher total dose of anti-psychotic medication than was intended. All SOADs have been made aware of the guidance from the Royal College of Psychiatrists (1993) on high doses of anti-psychotics, which was discussed in the last Biennial Report (5.7). Increasingly, SOADs are recording PRN medication specifically on Forms 39 and they are also being urged to time-limit their certificates when an early progress report under Section 61 (see 5.2.3) appears advisable.

As well as arranging training sessions for SOADs newly appointed during this reporting period, the Commission has held SOAD seminars in Nottingham, Bristol and Chester on *The ECT Handbook* of the Royal College of Psychiatrists (1995). The Commission is considering ways in which to ensure that this Handbook's recommendations are adopted.

5.2.3 Monitoring of Consent Forms and Reports

Forms 39

The Commission receives copies of all completed Forms 39 as well as a detailed report on each visit from its appointed SOADs. These are examined by clinically qualified members of the Commission's Consent to Treatment Group. The monitoring process is primarily designed to identify errors and omissions on Forms 39. The Forms and accompanying reports also provide information about non-consenting patients and occasionally about the milieu in which they are treated. SOAD reports are sometimes a useful pointer to issues requiring the attention of Commission members on forthcoming Visits.

The Commission has sought legal advice on the correction of forms found to contain errors which come to light both through its own monitoring and through the vigilance of Mental Health Act Administrators and other staff at the units concerned. The provisions of Section 15 of the Act about the correction of statutory forms do not apply to Consent to Treatment forms. The Commission has been advised that minor errors (such as misspelling of names) may be corrected, preferably by the SOAD, as long as it is clear that the requirements of Section 58 have been met. Treatment cannot be lawfully given if a Form 39 contains major errors or is incomplete. A further SOAD visit has to be arranged, for example, if the record shows failure to comply with a requirement of the Act, such as absence of a second consultee.

Progress Reports under Section 61

Under Section 61, progress reports on treatments authorized by SOADs are required to be sent to the Commission when an unrestricted patient's detention is renewed or, for restricted patients, when the RMO submits a statutory report to the Home Secretary. These reports are also monitored by the Commission's Consent to Treatment Group, allowing the Commission to check that a patient's current treatment is within that authorized by the most recent Form 39.

> **Hithergreen Hospital, Lewisham & Guys Mental Health NHS Trust: SOAD visit 18.6.96**
>
> Treatment with an anti-psychotic medication by depot injection <u>or</u> by mouth had been authorized by a SOAD on Form 39. A subsequent Section 61 report indicated that the patient was receiving depot anti-psychotic medication <u>as well as</u> a regular oral dose. A further Second Opinion was arranged.

The Commission regularly encounters examples of authorized treatments being exceeded. This is not only unlawful but also deprives the patient of the safeguard of a Second Opinion. The Commission is always ready to arrange a further Second Opinion if an RMO wishes to change the treatment plan from that authorized.

Monitoring Section 61 reports also allows the Commission to withdraw certificates when treatment has been discontinued or to arrange a further SOAD visit when necessary. It is the Commission's current policy that no certificate should run for over two years. For patients in high-security units, or for those who have high-dose or complex treatment plans, this limit is reduced to one year. If there are questions about the treatment it may be decided by either the Commission or the SOAD that this period should be considerably shorter.

The Code of Practice (16.21b) requires that a copy of the Section 61 report is given to the patient, but this recommendation is widely and regrettably disregarded.

5.2.4 The Independence of SOADs

Some patients, and indeed some mental health professionals, have expressed scepticism of the independence, in practice, of Second Opinion Appointed Doctors. During the period under review the Commission has been recording the number of occasions when the treatment plan of an RMO is amended prior to treatment being authorized under Section 58 by the SOAD. Amendments had occurred in 15% of all cases.

At a hospital in Southern England a SOAD was called in November 1995 to a 39 year old patient with a long history of schizophrenia that was resistant to treatment. He had been detained under Section 3 for five years and was described as 'tormented by delusions'. The RMO wanted to administer three regular anti-psychotic drugs (including clozaril) with a fourth drug available for intra-muscular administration in emergency. In addition, the RMO wanted to add a new anti-psychotic, not yet in the BNF. The SOAD, who had seen the patient before, contacted the manufacturer of the new drug and was advised that data on its use when combined with established anti-psychotic medication was not available. Following discussion, a Form 39 was issued for a treatment plan in which two drugs were withdrawn before introducing the new agent.

At a London hospital in November 1996 a 32 year old female patient with a long history of recurrent mania was seen by a SOAD at the end of the three month period of initial treatment. The plan included continuation of a calcium channel blocking agent, licensed for the treatment of cerebral ischaemia following sub-arachnoid haemorrhage. Some clinical reports had suggested that it might be useful also for rapid cycling manic disorder. After discussion between the RMO and SOAD it was agreed that the continued use of this drug for a detained patient incapable of consent was inappropriate under Section 58. A modified treatment plan was agreed.

The above example highlights, not only the type of modification that might be made as a consequence of a SOAD visit, but also the issue of using unestablished treatments for detained patients. This was referred to in the last Biennial Report (5.17) and is discussed fully in the Commission's Position Paper *Research and Detained Patients*, published in 1997.

5.2.5 Problems Encountered on SOAD Visits

SOADs continue to report difficulty at times in locating a second professional, other than a doctor or nurse, for consultation about treatment as required by Section 58 (Code of Practice 16.34b). Although the Commission reminds RMOs that it is their responsibility to nominate and arrange for the presence of the statutory consultees, the failure to do so can, unfortunately, sometimes be compounded by the actions of the SOAD.

Queen Elizabeth II Hospital, East Hertfordshire NHS Trust: SOAD Visit Feb. 1996.

In order to fulfil the requirements of the Act, a Form 39 authorizing ECT was signed by a SOAD using a hospital secretary as a person "professionally concerned" with the patient's treatment. A locum consultant subsequently questioned the validity of the form, which was withdrawn by the Commission and a further SOAD visit arranged.

Not all apparently unacceptable consultees turn out to be so. The validity of a hospital pharmacist has been challenged. Where, as at hospitals like Rampton High Security Hospital, the pharmacist has had contact with the patient and has been involved in discussions of the case at clinical ward rounds, such consultation clearly falls within the provisions of the Act. If there is doubt about a person's suitability to be a consultee it should be noted that this is not only a decision for the RMO and the SOAD, but also for the nominated consultee who should be satisfied that he or she is suitably qualified and adequately and professionally involved in the patient's care before agreeing to fill this statutory role (Code of Practice, 16.3.5).

5.2.6 Complaints Concerning Second Opinions

It was stated in the last Biennial Report (5.18) that the number of complaints about Second Opinions is relatively small. This continues to be the case. Ten complaints relating to Second Opinions have been received over this period, of which five have been upheld or partially upheld. One complaint is still under investigation. Six complaints were made by patients, one was made by a Social Worker and three were made by the same RMO against three different SOADs.

The decision of a SOAD cannot be the subject of an appeal to the Commission, but in response to a patient's complaint the Commission can call for a report under Section 61 and, if it so wishes, can withdraw a certificate issued by a SOAD. The Commission has a formal procedure for investigating complaints about Second Opinion visits.

Complaints from patients continue to be about perceived shortfalls in the consultation process. Two such complaints were partially upheld in this period; one because the SOAD arrived to see the patient at the unacceptably late hour of 9 pm and the other because the SOAD, who was not supplied with a translator for a patient unable to speak English, had seen but not interviewed the patient on his visit. In both cases, the Commission apologised to the patients concerned and, in the latter case, a further visit was arranged. Complaints were referred back to the hospital when they included matters under the hospital's control.

Two of the three complaints received from the RMO were that a SOAD had not consulted him while making a Second Opinion visit, in one instance leading to an error in the authorized treatment plan. The Commission advises SOADs that, however clearly the treatment plan is recorded, consultation with the RMO is expected (Code of Practice 16.27), if only by telephone where a face to face consultation is not possible. The third RMO complaint was that a Form 39 resulting from a SOAD visit did not comply with the Commission's own guidelines. All three of these complaints were upheld.

5.2.7 Urgent Treatment under Section 62

Section 62 of the Act authorizes the administration in an emergency of treatment that would normally require consent or a Second Opinion under the provisions of Section 58. The Commission is producing a Guidance Note on the use of this Section which will include a model record form to meet the requirements of the Code of Practice (16.19).

Only those patients who are detained under Sections to which Part IV of the Act applies can be given treatment under the authority of Section 62. The Commission, nevertheless, continues to receive reports of treatment administered under the purported authority of this Section to patients detained under Sections 4 and 5 or, on occasion, to patients not detained at all.

The Commission is concerned that the facility of giving emergency treatment should not be used when a Second Opinion could be obtained promptly.

> **St Anne's Hospital, Poole, Dorset NHS Trust: SOAD visit August 1996**
>
> An informal patient was refusing food and drink, was dehydrated and was detained under Section 5(2). The patient was not capable of giving consent, so the RMO authorized the use of ECT under common law and provided a recommendation for the implementation of Section 2. Believing that the formalities had been completed, the RMO requested a SOAD visit with a view to authorizing further ECT. The ASW assessing the patient for admission under Section 2 had found the patient "muddled" from the after-effects of ECT and had declined to sign the application form until the following day. On arrival the SOAD found no completed application form, no recorded treatment plan and no 'other professional' available for consultation and therefore could not give the Second Opinion requested. Because of the postponement of the SOAD's examination a second ECT was administered under Section 62 following the implementation of Section 2.

5.2.8 Other Treatments without Consent (Section 63)

Those forms of medical treatment for mental disorder given under the direction of the RMO that do not fall under either Section 57 or 58 may fall under the provisions of Section 63, for which the consent of the patient is not required. Section 63 can only be used to authorize treatment for patients who are detained under a Section to which Part IV of the Act applies. There have been a number of recent judicial decisions which have implications for the operation of Section 63, seeming to favour a wider interpretation of this Section than appeared to be intended when the Act was drafted.

In *B v Croydon Health Authority [1995] 2 W.L.R. 294*, it was ruled that 'ancillary acts' (in this case naso-gastric feeding for a patient refusing to eat) necessary to prevent patients causing harm to themselves or to prevent deterioration in their condition were lawful under Section 63. In *Tameside & Glossop Acute Services Trust v CH (a patient) [1996] 1 F.L.R. 762*, the court ruled that the induction of labour and, if necessary, a caesarian section was allowable without the patient's consent on the grounds that the course of the mental disorder might otherwise be adversely affected.

The Commission is concerned that recent judgements have been misleadingly reported in the press and could be inappropriately applied in practice. It intends, therefore, to produce a Guidance Note on the use of Section 63.

The eating disorder, anorexia nervosa, raises particular problems and the Commission has produced a Guidance Note (No. 3) to help clarify the issues. Only in its most severe manifestations can it be considered a life-threatening mental disorder requiring compulsory admission under the Mental Health Act. The Commission's view, supported by much psychiatric opinion, is that detention is justified in rare cases of serious threat to health, where compulsory feeding may be necessary to combat both the physical complications and the underlying mental disorder. However, in conformity with the principle of applying the least restrictive alternative, the Commission recommends regular multi-disciplinary review and the discontinuation of artificial feeding as soon as is practicable.

The Commission recommends that, in the light of cases involving the naso-gastric feeding of detained patients in the absence of their consent and under the authority of the Act, naso-gastric feeding should be regulated by the provisions of Section 58. This would provide the safeguard of a Second Opinion.

5.3 Treatment Requiring Consent and a Second Opinion

Section 57 stipulates that before the treatments that fall within its provisions can be administered to any prospective patient, a registered medical practitioner and two lay persons appointed by the Commission must certify that the patient is capable of understanding the nature, purpose and likely effects of the treatment and consents to it, and the registered medical practitioner must further certify that the treatment is likely to alleviate or prevent a deterioration in the patient's condition and that it should be given.

The treatments in question are the surgical implantation of hormones to reduce male sexual drive and any surgical operation for destroying brain tissue or for destroying its function. No cases in the former category have been referred under Section 57 since the last Biennial Report. The latter category is commonly but loosely referred to as 'psychosurgery', but in accordance with the recommendations of the recent CRAG

(Clinical Resource and Audit Group) Report (1996) (see 5.3.1), the Commission has adopted the more precise term of 'Neurosurgery for Mental Disorder ' (NMD).

Between 1 July 1995 and 31 March 1997, 30 visits for Section 57 assessments of proposed NMD have been undertaken, all of them leading to authorization of an operation. All but one of the operations had taken place by the end of this reporting period. One visit was a second referral where, on the first occasion, the Commission appointed team did not authorize treatment. One visit was a third referral, also of a case not previously authorized, where the patient had withdrawn her consent on the first two occasions. Referrals have been for 13 male and 14 female patients, for either affective disorders or obsessional disorders and for patients ranging in age from young adults to persons over seventy years.

Section 57 applies to any prospective NMD operation regardless of whether the patient is detained under the Act. In this reporting period a detained patient has been referred for the first time since the introduction of the Act. The patient received certification and subsequent reports have indicated a favourable outcome, including improved intellectual performance attributed to improved mood and concentration, despite continuing mental disorder.

NMD operations by operating centre:

University Hospital of Wales	17
Kings College Hospital	8
Brook Hospital	1
Pinderfields Hospital	2
National Hospital for Neurology and Neurosurgery	1

The sharp decrease in referrals noted in the Sixth Biennial Report seems to have levelled off. The decrease in referrals may be largely due to the enforced inactivity of the Geoffrey Knight Unit during 1995 and the early part of 1996. In late 1994 the radioactive yttrium, used uniquely by this Unit, went out of production and the Unit moved location before restarting operations using radio-frequency for the lesion. The operating centre for this Unit has now moved from the Brook Hospital to Kings College Hospital.

Three patients treated at Cardiff were referred for second operations, the first operations having failed to achieve the desired result either in the relief of symptoms or in producing a lesion of adequate size. In each case a very full review of the circumstances was conducted and authorization was given.

The Commission requires progress reports on treatment under Section 61 six months following NMD operations. This means that the report is usually submitted by the doctor in charge of the continuing treatment of the patient. The Commission recognises that it is difficult to evaluate outcomes of NSM and will be preparing a structured form to assist doctors making these reports. A letter to the patient will be included asking them to complete a self-report form if they wish. The Commission will also remind doctors who refer cases that the furnishing of Section 61 reports is a legal requirement. The Commission recommends that the neuro-surgeon undertaking the operation be routinely involved in any follow-up assessments.

5.3.1 Recommendations on Neurosurgery for Mental Disorder from the Scottish Office

The Commission contributed to an important review of NMD undertaken by the Scottish Office. The resulting *Neurosurgery for Mental Disorder* report of the CRAG (Clinical Resource and Audit Group) Working Group on Mental Illness (July 1996) recommends the introduction of standardised protocols for NMD and a systematic audit of the results of NMD in the United Kingdom by the Royal College of Psychiatrists. The Commission strongly endorses these proposals.

The CRAG report also proposes a mechanism for authorizing surgical treatment on patients for whom it is clinically indicated and who do not object to surgery, but who cannot give valid consent because of the severity of their condition. In Scotland the authorization would only be by the Courts. In England and Wales the Mental Health Act precludes surgical intervention in such cases. The Commission will be studying the implementation of the CRAG proposals and their effects before recommending any changes to the Act.

The CRAG report also recommends that the assessment of capacity and consent prior to NMD be undertaken some months before the proposed operation date. This has not been the practice in England and Wales, where operation dates have previously often been dictated by the availability of short-life radioactive yttrium which was used to create the lesion. As yttrium is no longer used in NSM this is no longer a consideration. The Commission considers that there are many advantages in planning for assessment earlier than has been the practice, particularly as Commission appointees, the clinicians and especially the patients have at times felt under pressure because of the proximity of assessment to the operation date. The Commission will therefore aim to make visits for Section 57 assessments earlier in the referral procedure. However, furnishing a certificate earlier does not preclude the patient from withdrawing consent at any time. Re-certification would then be needed should the patient later want to proceed.

5.3.2 Referrals From Overseas

There have been overseas referrals in the reporting period for patients from Australia, Eire and the USA. Some difficulties arise in meeting the requirements of the Act for such referrals, particularly the obligation to consult a nurse and another person professionally concerned with the patient's treatment before authorization. There have also been problems in the Commission's appointees gaining access to all relevant clinical records. However, in the case of Eire, it was possible, by special arrangement with the relevant Health Authorities, for the Commission team to visit and to assess the patient in a local hospital.

Identifying the doctor who is in charge of the treatment for purposes of the Act and who must provide subsequent reports is sometimes a problem, particularly for referrals from overseas. Difficulties arise when incomplete information is presented and when arrangements are made at short notice.

5.3.3 Consent to a Plan of Treatment

The Commission has been given early notice of an intention to re-introduce multifocal leuco-coagulation, a progressive form of neuro-surgery for mental disorder developed in Bristol. This involves insertion of a sheath of electrodes into the brain which are progressively stimulated to destroy tissue, gradually increasing the size of the lesion until a therapeutic effect is produced. The total procedure might take some months. The question arises whether a certificate is required for each stage, or whether one would satisfy legal requirements, on the understanding that the patient could withdraw consent at any stage under the provisions of Section 60. The Commission has received legal advice that, since the Act and form of authorization refers to a plan of treatment, one certificate should remain valid throughout the procedure.

Chapter 6

Complaints

Summary

The Commission's remit to investigate complaints from patients about matters which occurred while detained under the Act ordinarily begins only after the complaint has been investigated by hospital managers and the patient remains dissatisfied with the outcome. Consequently, the Commission mounts a formal investigation itself in only a small minority of the complaints brought to its attention. It more often performs a monitoring function, ensuring that patients are clear about the issues they want pursued and that they receive consideration and response from managers. A Commission investigation may sometimes need to be postponed pending the outcome of an independent review under the new NHS complaints procedure, but the policy to postpone in all such cases has been reconsidered in the light of the possibility of damaging delays.

Complaints mostly concern detention or medical care, services and treatment. Complaints from High Security Hospitals highlight matters noted during Visits, such as access to fresh air, availability of escorts and delays in reports to Tribunals and the Home Office. The Commission no longer excludes the investigation of complaints about clinical judgement.

A comparatively large number of complaints are received from some Mental Nursing Homes, which causes particular concern when managers rarely acknowledge that the patient's comments have any foundation.

6 Complaints

6.1 The Remit

The Commission's remit to investigate complaints is set out in Section 120 (1)b of the Mental Health Act 1983. The Commission may investigate two types of complaint:

- any complaint made by a person in respect of a matter which occurred while he was detained under the Act, and which has not been dealt with to his satisfaction by the managers of the hospital or registered mental nursing home.

- any other complaint as to the exercise of powers and discharge of duties conferred or imposed by the Act in respect of a detained patient.

The Commission need not investigate all complaints coming within its jurisdiction and may discontinue an investigation where it is considered appropriate to do so. Where the Commission undertakes an investigation, a Commission member is entitled to visit and interview any patient and inspect any records relating to that person's detention or care.

The work of the Commission under this remit is important because each complaint received means that a patient or relative is sufficiently troubled to make the effort to find out how to complain and to approach the Commission in writing, by telephone or at an interview during a Commission Visit. For detained patients this requires a degree of motivation and initiative that must be reflected in the quality of the response they receive.

Complaints provide a useful indicator of care standards. Where complaints are unusually frequent they can sometimes point to possible deficiencies in the units concerned and highlight matters to be given priority during subsequent Commission Visits.

Revised procedures for dealing with complaints, introduced throughout the NHS and which were referred to in the Sixth Biennial Report (4.8), became effective on 1 April 1996. These changes are intended to lead to a more consistent way of dealing with complaints, with Trusts standardising their procedures and paying greater attention to response times.

Under this new system, hospital managers are expected to respond to a formal complaint and achieve a local resolution if possible. If patients are not satisfied with this response they can ask for an Independent Review. Such requests are considered by a Complaints Convenor appointed by the Trust (usually a Non-Executive Director). The Complaints Convenor can refuse the request or ask for further information or further attempts at local resolution. If it is intended to set up an Independent Review Panel, the Complaints Convenor must consult the independent chairperson of the Panel, who may also ask for further information or suggest further ways of seeking local resolution. Although extending patients' rights, the effect of this new step in the procedure is to introduce the potential for substantial delay in the resolution of complaints.

If patients remain dissatisfied, either because an Independent Review has been refused or after their complaint has been considered and responded to by the Panel, they can then ask the Commission or the Health Service Commissioner to investigate.

By arrangement between the Commission and the Health Service Commissioner's office, the Commission may investigate such cases first, but the patient retains the right to appeal to the Health Service Commissioner subsequently if dissatisfied with the outcome of the Commission's investigation.

It has been the Commission's policy not to investigate complaints until after the Independent Review stage, but because of the possibility of serious delay affecting the outcome of investigations, the Commission has decided to use its discretion in considering whether to investigate a complaint without waiting for the response to a request for Independent Review. These decisions will be influenced by the seriousness of the complaint and they will be exercised with caution and subject to review.

In parallel with the remit of the Health Service Commissioner, the Mental Health Act Commission will no longer exclude consideration of complaints about clinical judgement when deciding whether to investigate a complaint. This allows detained patients to make complaints not only about the way procedures under the Act have been carried out or about the conditions under which they are detained, but also about professional decisions regarding their clinical care and treatment.

6.2   Administrative Changes

As reported in the Sixth Biennial Report, the Commission's work on complaints has been re-organised and centralised at the head office in Nottingham. A small, dedicated administrative team has been created to provide speedy and consistent responses to complaints. Records of complaints are now maintained on a database. This has greatly improved the information available, enabled the progress of individual complaints to be properly monitored and provided Commission members with particulars of complaints from the units they are visiting.

A Commission member appointed as Complaints Coordinator oversees the work of the Unit, deals with the more complex cases and makes decisions about which cases should be investigated by the Commission. A small team of Complaints Investigators has been appointed to carry out this work.

The Commission carries out a formal investigation of its own in only a small minority of the complaints notified to it, more often it undertakes a monitoring role, where necessary asking hospitals to investigate further particular issues which the Commission, or the complainant, regard as having had a less than full and satisfactory response. It is possible that requests for the Commission to mount investigations may increase if the outcomes of Independent Reviews currently in progress do not satisfy complainants.

6.3   Processing of Complaints

Complaints are sometimes brought to the attention of members of the Commission during hospital Visits. These complaints are referred at the time (with the patient's consent) to the hospital managers for action. During their interviews with detained patients, Commission members can help them to clarify their complaints, which can often be set out in the letter summarising the interview, a copy of which goes to the ward manager. Thereafter, the complaint is pursued by the Commission only if the patient reports that they have had no response or are dissatisfied with the response received.

The majority of complaints to the Commission are received by letter or telephone call and dealt with by the Complaints Unit. Patients are advised of the need to refer to hospital managers in the first instance, but complaints can be forwarded on their behalf if they do not wish to do so themselves. Confidentiality is paramount and patients must be given the opportunity to say that they do not wish their complaints to go before hospital managers.

Some detained patients may not pursue their concerns through the hospital complaints system, particularly if these involve implicit criticism of staff, because they fear that by doing so they could jeopardise their future care or prospects of discharge. In such cases, Commission members do their best to reassure and encourage patients. If this is not successful, they try to draw attention to the issues in a general way, without identifying the patient.

Where a complaint concerns an alleged failure in the exercise of powers or the discharge of duties under the Act, the Commission may investigate without requiring the complainant (who may be a third party) to take up matters first with the hospital managers. It is, however, the Commission's practice generally to seek first a response from the unit concerned before deciding whether to conduct its own investigation.

The Act gives the Commission discretion to decline to conduct an investigation or to discontinue an investigation which has begun. In practice, decisions are determined by such considerations as the quality of the investigation by the hospital managers, the seriousness of the complaint and the prospect of acquiring further relevant evidence (having regard to the time elapsed, witness availability etc.).

Where the Commission does undertake a full enquiry, it may examine medical, nursing and Social Services records and interview the complainant and other persons concerned, but it cannot compel witnesses to come forward. The Commission subsequently provides a written report to the complainant which is copied to the Trust or Mental Nursing Home.

6.4   Complaints from Relatives Concerning the Death of a Detained Patient

The limitations imposed by the Commission's complaints remit can lead to frustration for relatives of detained patients who have died. Whereas the Commission can investigate any aspect of care and treatment when a complaint has been made by a detained patient and where the patient is dissatisfied with the response by hospital managers, it cannot do so when a complaint about aspects of care and treatment is made by a relative or other third party.

The Commission's remit in these cases is limited by statute to investigating "the exercise of the powers or the discharge of the duties conferred or imposed by this Act" (the Mental Health Act). This definition excludes matters relating to care and treatment and as complaints from relatives almost invariably are about aspects of care rather than about whether the provisions of the Act are complied with, a great deal of frustration is caused to all concerned.

Since the patient in such cases is no longer able to make a complaint about these matters, it could be argued that such an interpretation of the Act denies concerned relatives the opportunity of having them investigated by the Commission under its complaints' remit.

6.5   Complaint Statistics

In March 1997, 129 complaints were currently being processed by the Complaints Unit, 6 of which were under formal investigation by the Commission.

A summary of the 1,100 complaints made to the Commission over a 21 month period between July 1995 and March 1997 is shown in Figure 10.

Figure 10: Complaints by category (n=1100)

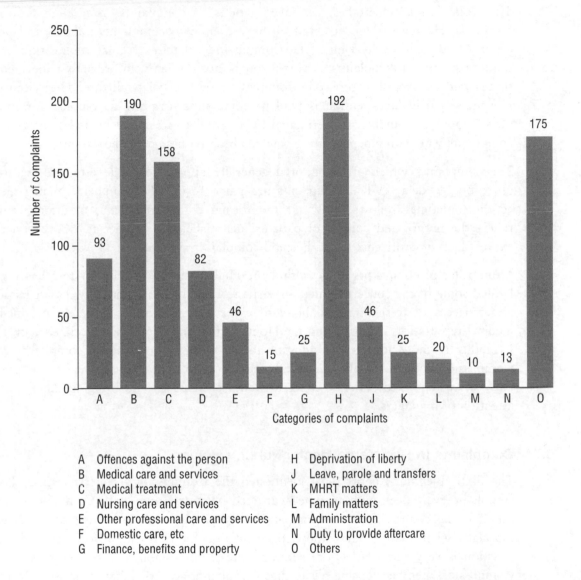

A   Offences against the person
B   Medical care and services
C   Medical treatment
D   Nursing care and services
E   Other professional care and services
F   Domestic care, etc
G   Finance, benefits and property

H   Deprivation of liberty
J   Leave, parole and transfers
K   MHRT matters
L   Family matters
M   Administration
N   Duty to provide aftercare
O   Others

These show that complaints against detention, medical care and services and medical treatment are the principal causes of concern, a pattern similar to that already noted in the analysis of issues raised by patients on Commission Visits (see 2.3).

6.6   Complaints in High Security Hospitals

The Commission undertakes few investigations of complaints from High Security Hospitals. However, these hospitals all have their own complaints policies and procedures and Complaints Units. The Commission organises regular monitoring of a random sample of complaints passing through those systems. In order to achieve continuity and an overall picture, one Commission member visits all three High Security Hospitals. Particular attention is paid to complaints awaiting a response for more than 2 months, complaints investigated by external or independent investigators and complaints where an independent review has been requested by the patient.

The complaints which are monitored generally appear to be investigated without unreasonable delay. When complaints are partially or wholly upheld, management action sometimes follows. How far the formal complaints being monitored truly reflect the nature and volume of patients' dissatisfactions is unclear. Many patients express lack of confidence in the hospital complaints system.

Monitoring of complaints made within the High Security Hospital system has highlighted some of the concerns noted on Visits to these hospitals, notably dissatisfaction about access to fresh air, availability of escorts for activities, delays in producing medical reports for Tribunals and the Home Office and problems associated with the Disability Living Allowance. In addition to the formal monitoring of complaints, the Commission activities at these hospitals include a considerable amount of time spent on Visits listening to patients' concerns about such issues and bringing them to the attention of managers.

6.7   Complaints in Registered Mental Nursing Homes

The Sixth Biennial Report (4.4) mentioned the Commission's concerns about how complaints were dealt with at some Registered Nursing Homes. The Commission continues to be concerned at the comparatively large number of complaints received, especially when managerial acknowledgement of some justification for patient dissatisfaction is very rare. Patients at some private sector establishments continue to tell Commission members during Visits that complaints are not taken seriously enough, which deters them from making a complaint. On occasion, the Commission has reported this to senior hospital managers.

6.8   Complaints against Commission Members and SOADS

There have been no complaints against members of the Commission in the period under review. Complaints involving SOADs have been discussed earlier (see 5.2.6).

6.9 Cases of Interest

The small minority of complaints that lead to formal investigation by the Commission tend to arise from unusual and complex circumstances, which may involve several issues.

Example I

The Complaint

A law centre, on behalf of a female patient, made a number of complaints alleging that she:

a) had been detained improperly under Section 4;

b) had been administered medication unlawfully in the absence of consent more than three months after treatment under detention had begun;

c) had been wrongly secluded when a suicide risk;

d) was strip searched by two female and three male nurses without respect for her dignity and privacy;

e) was not provided with clean sanitary protection or underwear for 40 minutes following a strip search;

f) was unlawfully detained, the social work assessment having been carried out later than shown on the official documentation.

The Investigation

The hospital managers' investigation considered complaints a) to e), which had been referred in November 1994. After some prompting, a response was received on 22nd March 1995. The patient stated that she was not interviewed about her complaints, nor asked for any further details. She was dissatisfied and, on 25th July 1995, the Commission was asked to investigate and agreed to do so.

The Commission's investigator interviewed the complainant, 11 members of the hospital staff and the ASW from the local Social Services Department. All relevant medical and other documentation was examined.

Conclusion

The Commission concluded that:

a) the use of Section 4 for admission had been appropriate in the light of the patient's history of self-harm, which included a near-fatal overdose;

b) there was no evidence to show that medication had been administered without her consent;

c) it had been wrong to seclude a patient who was a known suicide risk; the care plan had specified seclusion "if necessary", contrary to guidance in the Code of Practice (18.15) that "seclusion is not a treatment technique and should not feature in any treatment programme";

d) the complaints about strip searching would be upheld;

e) the complaint about being left with soiled sanitary protection and no underwear would be upheld;

f) the complaint that the ASW assessment was later than indicated on the documentation would be upheld.

The outcome was an apology to the patient from the Trust, a review and amendment of the Trust's seclusion policy and the provision of further guidance and training for staff.

Example II

The Complaint

The father of a patient who died whilst detained under the Act complained to the Commission that his son:

a) whilst remanded to hospital for assessment under Section 35 of the Act, and in an Intensive Care Unit (ICU), was prematurely transferred back to prison without the assessment being completed and without enquiries being made of available alternatives to a remand to prison;

b) was placed in a strip cell at one prison and was then transferred to a remand facility at another prison, wholly inappropriate to his needs, where he committed suicide.

The Investigation

Complaint (a) was referred to the hospital managers by the Commission on behalf of the complainant. Complaint (b) did not fall within the NHS complaint procedures.

The managers examined relevant medical notes and interviewed all the staff involved and established the following points.

After three weeks of assessment it had been concluded that the patient required extended treatment in a structured environment, but it was considered that he could not be contained in the ICU. As immediate action was required, he was referred back to the courts for the revocation of Section 35 and transfer to prison, with a view to ongoing transfer to a Regional Secure Unit (RSU).

No referral had been made earlier to that RSU as it had been considered initially that the patient could be fully assessed at the ICU and with a view to being treated in a more conducive environment than the RSU. It was also believed that direct referral to the RSU could not be achieved from the ICU.

The Commission investigated the complaint. The Commission's investigator spoke with the complainant and interviewed staff at the hospital and also examined medical documentation and other papers, including a transcript of the Inquest.

Conclusion

It was confirmed that the Trust was at fault in making no approach to the local RSU or to other RSUs. The Trust had assumed that there would be an extensive waiting list at the local RSU and that access to the others was barred to psychiatric units outside their immediate area of operation. It seemed likely that the developing role of the Trust's ICU as a Forensic Unit may have led to a lack of clarity about its inter-relationship with the local RSU.

The complaint was upheld.

The Commission recommended that a protocol of good practice for mentally disordered offenders should be established, with particular regard to the inter-relationship between the ICU and the local RSU.

In the majority of instances the Commission's role is necessarily limited (see 6.1).

Example III

The Complaint

A patient alleged that whilst detained in a Mental Nursing Home as a remand prisoner under Section 48/49 of the Act he did not see a "psychologist or anyone" and was left alone for five weeks without receiving any help or treatment.

The Investigation

The hospital managers investigated, seeking information from the patient's RMO and members of the nursing staff. It was established that the patient had had extensive contact with his RMO and with staff of various disciplines while he was detained. A psychologist had attempted to make contact with him on two occasions, but both times he had been engaged in other activities.

The Commission forwarded the original letter of complaint to the hospital managers on the patient's behalf, requesting an investigation be carried out and a report forwarded to the patient and the Commission. On receipt of the report the Commission corresponded with the patient, advising that he should take legal advice regarding the claim he wished to make against the hospital. An offer to forward comments to the hospital on the patient's behalf was declined.

Conclusion

The patient did not respond to subsequent correspondence and the file was closed.

The Commission's role in this case was to ensure that the complaint was sent to the managers, that a written report of an investigation was received and that the patient had access to further advice following the managers' investigation.

The fact that the Commission considers a complaint sufficiently substantial to warrant a formal investigation does not mean that it will ultimately be upheld.

Example IV

The Complaint

A patient alleged that whilst detained in a Mental Nursing Home under Section 37/41 of the Act, visits from his fiancee to see him on the ward had been prohibited by his consultant and he was also denied leave to meet her in the grounds of the hospital.

The Investigation

The hospital managers investigated, seeking information from the patient's RMO and the clinical team and also considering the findings of his most recent Mental Health Review Tribunal six months earlier. They advised the patient that the decisions about which he had complained had resulted from the fact that his fiancee had also been a patient on the ward where he was detained and that he had not qualified for escorted leave in the hospital grounds. They pointed out that when he did qualify for such leave, he could meet with his fiancee in the grounds by arrangement. The patient was not satisfied with this response and requested assistance from the Commission.

The Commission's investigator asked the hospital managers to provide details of the patient's care plan, including future plans for escorted or unescorted leave.

Conclusion

The Commission concluded that:

a)   the care plan provided for escorted leave to take place and full reasons were given for current restrictions;

b)   the RMO had acted within the powers conferred by the Act, taking into account the patient's assessed needs and previous behaviour.

The complaint was not upheld.

Chapter 7

Deaths

Summary

The Commission has established a small team of specifically trained members, working alongside the Complaints Unit, to review deaths of detained patients, over 350 of which are reported to the Commission annually. Clear criteria will be established for deciding which deaths should be reviewed in depth by the Commission.

When a detained patient dies suddenly or in untoward circumstances, questions may be asked, for example, about the quality of care accorded patients at risk of self-harm, the adequacy of documentation and performance in relation to patients under special observation, the effectiveness of medical cover, the monitoring of high dosage medication or the control of aggressive behaviour.

Deaths of detained patients while on Section 17 leave or absent without leave call into question the adequacy of procedures for authorizing leave, informing relatives and checking times of return as well as the undertaking of prompt and appropriate action in cases of unauthorized absence.

7 Deaths

7.1 Enquiries into Deaths of Detained Patients

7.1.1 The Commission's Policy Review

The Sixth Biennial Report set out the Commission's continuing interest in and concerns about the deaths of detained patients (6.2). Following an analysis of findings from inquests attended by Commission members (Banerjee et al, 1995) and referred to in the last Biennial Report (6.0), the Commission has reviewed the way in which it pursues its statutory responsibilities in relation to patients who die whilst detained. A new policy, endorsed by Ministers, has been circulated to Trusts, Health Authorities and Registered Mental Nursing Homes and came into force on February 1st 1997.

Commission activity in relation to the deaths of detained patients is now managed centrally, alongside the work of the Complaints Unit. This will facilitate a consistent approach by the Commission and the development of clear criteria for deciding which deaths should be reviewed in depth. The systematic collection of data on deaths of detained patients enables the Commission to identify both good and bad practice and share any lessons learnt with those who commission and deliver mental health services.

7.1.2 The Commission's Remit

Where the Commission decides to review the circumstances surrounding the death of a detained patient its primary focus is the exercise of powers and discharge of duties under the Act and the implementation of the Code of Practice (see 6.4).

7.1.3 Previous Procedures

Prior to the implementation of the current policy, the Commission gathered information about deaths primarily by attending inquests, usually in the role of an observer. Decisions as to the categories of deaths investigated and the lines of follow-up pursued with the hospital or other authorities were made on a regional basis.

This approach is no longer considered adequate. Despite a longstanding request that all hospitals should report any death of a detained patient to the Commission, the fact and content of the notification was not always reliable or complete. In addition, despite a further request for notification of the inquest date by the hospital, the Commission would sometimes be given only a few days notice and, on occasion, would discover that the inquest had already taken place.

Additional problems often arose from the fact that inquests are sometimes held many months after the death and are primarily concerned to establish the immediate cause of death. Coroners are often reluctant to enquire into areas of poor practice, taking the view that this is a matter for the civil and criminal courts.

The lack of a central Commission Unit also hampered the dissemination of valuable information. Lessons learnt from the circumstances surrounding individual deaths were often confined to the Commission region concerned rather than the organisation generally.

7.1.4 The New Policy

The new policy calls for notification of deaths of detained patients to the Commission within 24 hours of the death. Units are asked to supply standard information which may not, at first sight, appear relevant to the cause of death, but which may signal the relevance of other factors. The Commission then decides on the priority to be accorded to each case. When thought necessary, a specialist Commission member will immediately visit the unit concerned to inspect the records and to be available to talk to staff and patients where appropriate.

Under the policy, a visit will be appropriate in circumstances including: apparent suicide; a recent history of seclusion; close observation or control and restraint; the administration of medication during or after a struggle; a high dosage or combination of drugs above British National Formulary limits. In addition, a Commission member should attend where a patient has died whilst on escorted leave or where they have sustained physical injuries. A visit may also be appropriate where death follows a medical condition with no apparent or adequate explanation.

Decisions as to whether to review further or to attend the inquest are made in the light of information from this preliminary visit or from the information provided on the initial Commission notification form. Copies of the relevant hospital records and internal reviews may be requested, and experts within the Commission membership may be consulted on particular issues, for example on the use of control and restraint, or the appropriate treatment for a particular physical medical condition. If necessary, advice may be sought from outside specialists.

As the centralised policy work develops, it will be possible to target particular areas of concern: a number of deaths may occur in an individual hospital, or a particular drug prescribing regime may be implicated nationally. A national data base should enable the Commission to produce more comprehensive statistics on deaths of detained patients than any other mental health agency.

7.1.5 Attending the Inquest as a Properly Interested Person

Commission members attending inquests have hitherto done so primarily as observers, although on occasion they have been invited to put questions. Negotiations are at present taking place with the Coroners' Society to recognise the Commission as a 'Properly Interested Person' in certain cases. Where it is felt that the Commission should make a more positive contribution to the proceedings under its new policy, an application would be made to the Coroner. The Commission's representative — normally a specialist member of the Commission itself — would, as a 'Properly Interested Person', be entitled to ask questions of witnesses and to ask for particular witnesses to attend court rather than their statements being read without questioning. It is envisaged that the Commission would seek such recognition rarely and only in the most serious cases.

The Commission would also be able to ask the Coroner to call additional witnesses and to consider lines of investigation which are often omitted after the deaths of detained patients, sometimes due to the lack of detailed knowledge of mental health issues on the part of those involved in the inquest process. Any specialist advice obtained by the Commission may also be submitted with a view to persuading the Coroner to call for expert evidence at the inquest.

The Commission will confine its involvement at the inquest to issues falling within its remit, recognising that the Coroner's own remit does not cover all its concerns. However, Coroners do have a duty to investigate areas beyond the mere physical cause of death and they have considerable discretion as to how far to broaden their inquiries.

7.1.6 Training and Resources

A number of Commission members have been selected and trained to investigate the deaths of detained patients. A Coroner has contributed to the training on matters concerning inquests. A Committee may be set up to oversee and monitor the investigatory work and to ensure that the Commission continues to develop and adapt its procedures in response to changing circumstances.

The work involved in extra visits to hospitals and attendance at inquests has resource implications for the Commission. Prior to the new policy, over 350 deaths of detained patients were reported annually to the Commission, far in excess of the number that can be investigated; after the first three months of the new policy's reporting requirements, the projected figure for 1997/98 is 400. The resources which the Commission is able to allocate to this aspect of its responsibilities are very limited and it will therefore have to be very selective about the cases which it reviews in depth.

7.2   Unexpected Deaths

Issues which arise when a patient commits suicide in hospital include the quality of care accorded to patients at risk of self-harm and the adequacy of documentation and performance in relation to patients under special observation. Suicides of patients while on leave authorised by the Responsible Medical Officer (under Section 17) often raise questions about the adequacy of the leave documentation (see 3.4) and about policies such as those covering risk assessment, communication with carers and the action to be taken when a patient fails to return at an agreed time.

Other unexpected deaths may raise questions about the adequacy of medical cover, including the care provided for physical complaints, especially for older people. The use of high dosage medication, polypharmacy and the possibility of adverse drug interactions are also areas of concern. Despite the Royal College of Psychiatrist's Consensus Statement on the use of neuroleptic medication (1993), highlighting the potential dangers of high dosages especially during or after a struggle, the details of deaths reported to the Commission indicate a continuing problem.

On occasion, as in the following example, evidence produced at an inquest points to obvious defects in procedures which need to be checked during subsequent Commission visits.

In January 1996 a patient in Marlborough House Medium Secure Unit, Milton Keynes Community NHS Trust, hanged herself in her bedroom during the night, using the cord from her dressing gown. She had arranged a bundle of clothes under her bedding to make it appear she was asleep to anyone shining a torch through the observation window of her room. She was well known as being at risk of self-harm and had been placed on periodic observations. There was some dispute as to whether the observations were to be at 5 or 15 minute intervals. The night staff apparently took it to be 15 minutes. Subsequent forensic examination of the case file established that the entry instructing 5 minutes had been changed in different ink to read 15.

This incident resulted in a thorough review by the unit of its policies and procedures, immediate and radical revision of the unit's observation policy and recording procedure and in the closer monitoring of its implementation, all of which were in place when the unit received its next Commission Visit.

7.3   Absence Without Leave

The Commission has emphasised the importance of maintaining and monitoring clear procedures when patients go absent without leave (see 3.4). This is essential to reduce the likelihood of serious incidents, notably suicide, violence to others and, of course, homicide. The number of suicides notified as having occurred while patients are absent without leave is a cause for serious concern and should lead hospitals to review their policies for keeping patients safe; a majority of deaths of patients while absent without leave occur within 24 hours of leaving the hospital premises.

Arrangements should be in place for making swift contact with relatives and GP in the event of a patient going absent without leave or failing to return from leave. It is also important for there to be a good working relationship with the police.

Missing Patients Procedures have been commented upon in a number of Inquiries into homicides by psychiatric patients (Blom-Cooper 1996; Mischon et al, 1995).

Chapter 8

Continuity of Care

Summary

Continuity of care is a key requirement of good practice. Although the Commission's remit does not extend to patients following discharge from detention, after-care planning while in hospital and Section 117 after-care meetings are of vital interest to patients and the Commission.

Implementation of the Care Programme Approach too often fails to meet standards set out in Trust policies. Attendance at Section 117 meetings by social workers and representatives of local agencies is often poor, especially when a patient has been cared for in a unit at a distance. Consultation with patients and their relatives about after-care arrangements needs to be improved.

There is still some need for clarification about charging for services provided under Section 117.

The Commission regrets that its remit has not been extended to cover Supervised Discharge. An opportunity to monitor the benefits and difficulties of the new power has been lost.

8 Continuity of Care

8.1 Legislative and Policy Framework

Two important statutory developments in community care have taken place since the Sixth Biennial Report. The implementation, in April 1996, of the Mental Health (Patients in the Community) Act 1995, introduced after-care under supervision, known as Supervised Discharge. The Carers (Recognition and Services) Act 1995 acknowledged the role of informal carers (usually relatives) and gave them the right to an assessment by the Local Authority to determine their ability to provide care. The provisions apply when a community assessment is being undertaken and the carer is providing, or intends to provide, a substantial amount of care on a regular basis.

The Government's objective to reduce ill-health and death caused by mental illness, was set out in *The Health of the Nation*. Community care initiatives intended to take this forward include the following:

- the development of standardised assessment scales (HONOS) to measure improvements in the health and social functioning of people with a mental illness;

- the publication of a guide, *Building Bridges*, describing good practice and emphasising continuity of care (Dept. of Health, 1995c);

- the publication of *The Spectrum of Care*, which sets out the range of hospital and local community care services required (Dept. of Health, 1996e);

- a 23% increase in The Mental Illness Specific Grant for 1996 to £58.3 million, with a further £9 million to be made available in 1997;

- the Mental Health Challenge Fund, supporting the development of new crisis intervention projects and the expansion of Community Mental Health Teams.

8.2   The Commission's Remit and Community Care.

The Commission's statutory remit is limited to patients who are detained or liable to be detained (e.g. those on Section 17 leave). In contrast, the remits of its sister Commissions in Scotland and Northern Ireland extend to all patients receiving treatment for mental disorder both in hospital and elsewhere. Nevertheless, community care is of vital interest to the detained patients seen on Commission Visits, when issues are frequently raised about their experiences before admission and their concern about what care they will have after leaving hospital.

Clearly, the success of hospital treatment will be affected by whether the community care available on discharge will meet the individual's needs. The main factors on which quality of care depends are adequate resources, effective collaboration between service providers and good communications with relevant local interest groups. During its joint Visits to providers of in-patient treatment and to Social Services Departments, the Commission takes note of patients' views and hears from professional staff about achievements and deficits in the provision of community care. Commission meetings with purchasers and representatives of voluntary agencies during Visits are additional sources of comment on how community care is working.

The Commission recognises an integrated approach to hospital and community care as a key requirement of good practice and commends innovative measures to promote it. If the links between hospital and community are weak, the chances of inappropriate admissions and inadequately planned discharges are greater. The continued involvement of community workers while their clients are in hospital, including attendance at review meetings, is to be encouraged. Smooth multi-disciplinary working is necessary to support all such arrangements.

A day hospital/home-based service can relieve pressure on hospital beds and encourage closer contacts between hospital and community staff. The Northern Birmingham Mental Health Services Trust, for example, has a rapid response team of psychiatrists and community psychiatric nurses to provide home-based care for acute disturbance. The provision of short-stay crisis and respite beds may be preferred by some patients and carers and could avoid the disruption of a period of detention under the Act. The availability of community support workers, able to give more intensive, practical support to users, is another welcome development in some areas.

The provision of a seamless service of continuous and interchangeable care is not without problems. It is evident that Community Mental Health Teams (CMHTs) face difficulties in reconciling competing demands on their time. Targeting resources on people with serious mental illness conflicts with continuing pressures from purchasers of primary health care for CMHT staff to meet the needs of other groups. This can lead to tensions between Social Services and Health Service staff in decisions about the allocation of key workers and other resources.

8.3 Section 117 and the Care Programme Approach (CPA)

All detained patients should benefit from the CPA, which is the cornerstone of individual care planning in England. The Commission is impressed by the commitment of Health and Social Services managers to its implementation. Progress has been made in integrating the obligations to provide after-care for detained patients under Section 117 within CPA provisions that are tiered according to assessed needs. However, those subject to Section 117 must be identifiable within the recording system and their particular requirements must not be overlooked.

Evidence from Commission Visits shows that in many areas CPA implementation is far from complete. There has been much activity in training of staff in CPA procedures, reflected in the number of CPA forms included in patients' files. In some areas practice is good, with timely care planning meetings involving patients and carers, leading to clear action plans. However, too often Commission members find practice failing to live up to agreed CPA policies. The following are some of the problems encountered.

- CPA forms are sometimes poorly designed and recording can be cumbersome, reducing staff commitment to the process as well as making it less user friendly for patients and carers.

- Some CPA forms do little to encourage the participation of patients and carers, when there is little or no space for their views and no place for them to sign to indicate their agreement or otherwise. The forms are frequently not fully completed or seemingly completed as a paper exercise without evidence of the participation of patients or carers.

- Care planning often occurs too late. Commission members still find examples of detained patients discharged without a multi-disciplinary Section 117 meeting or appearing at a Tribunal hearing without a Section 117 meeting having been arranged.

Some patients find large planning meetings intimidating and are unable to participate effectively; consequently their views and needs get overlooked. It is vital that professionals identify ways to show patients that their concerns are understood and taken into account in care planning.

Charing Cross Hospital, Riverside Mental Health Trust: Visit October 1996

Commissioners found patchy recording of after-care planning in the patients' notes. Comprehensive care plans, based on proper assessments and with clearly identified needs (Code of Practice 27.9) were not in evidence on most of those records. Three of the five patients seen on Ward A expressed concerns about future plans for them and often appeared to be unaware of what was being set up. The CPA documentation was largely blank apart from the demographic information on the front of the form. The care coordinator role was blank in all of the forms looked at. This was even the case where a patient had had several recent admissions.

8.4 Attendance at CPA and Section 117 Meetings

It is not easy to assemble the appropriate people to attend these meetings. Hospital staff sometimes report difficulty in securing the attendance of community staff, although this tends to be easier where there are established CMHTs. Lack of GP involvement is frequently reported and the Commission continues to hear complaints from some advocates and carers' groups that they are not informed of planning meetings. The Commission recommends that clear and timely information about the care planning process should be made available to patients and carers.

For patients in hospitals a long way from their home, where links with their home area have been disrupted, it is particularly important to have effective care planning involving family members and local professionals. Although it is customary to invite and expect local professionals to attend, other solutions may have to be sought (see 4.4.4)

8.5 Care Management

In most areas, proper integration of CPA and Section 117 with care management has yet to happen. Ideally, there should be local protocols for linking CPA and Section 117 care planning with procedures for assessment of community care needs and care management under the NHS and Community Care Act 1990. The Commission hopes for progress towards this end through local policy development so that patients can have the benefit of fully coordinated multi-disciplinary assessment and care planning.

The involvement of carers in after-care planning is an important aspect of the CPA and the Commission notes a gradual improvement in practice in this regard. It will be interesting to see what effect the new Carers (Recognition and Services) Act 1995 may have on after-care planning. It should encourage a more systematic approach to assessment of carers' ability to provide care and their need for support.

8.6   Charges for Section 117 After-Care

A question has arisen whether Local Authorities can charge patients who have been detained (under Sections 3, 37, 47 or 48) for the after-care provided to them in discharge of the obligations referred to in Section 117. A survey in the North West found that many Authorities distinguish between domicilary or day-care services and residential care, charging for the latter, for which the service user with limited means would normally be able to claim financial assistance from the Local Authority to offset the charges.

Legal opinion (citing a judgement in *McCarthy and Stone (Developments Ltd.) v Richmond-upon-Thames LBC* (1992) 2AC 48) suggests that Local Authorities can impose charges only where there is a statutory basis for doing so, which the Mental Health Act does not provide. This conclusion applies both to charges for residential and non-residential services and to charging patients while under Guardianship and Supervised Discharge.

Some uncertainties remain. People subject to Section 117 assessed under Section 47 of the NHS and Community Care Act as needing other services, not covered by their Section 117 package, may be charged for them. This leaves open to interpretation what should be regarded as part of Section 117 after-care and what services are for different needs arising from, for example, physical disability. According to the Act, the obligation imposed by Section 117 comes to an end, so free services cease, when both Local and Health Authorities are "satisfied that the person concerned is no longer in need of such services". How this decision is to be made is unclear. The Department of Health will be considering whether to issue guidance to clarify when charges can be made and to standardise Section 117 procedures across the country.

At the time of writing, draft policy and practice guidance under the Community Care (Direct Payments) Act 1996 was in the process of consultation. The Act will allow a Local Authority to make a payment to individuals, assessed as needing community care services, which they can use to secure the relevant services for themselves. However, the regulations made under the Act specifically exclude direct payments being offered to people subject to mental health and criminal justice legislation, who are required to receive specific community care services. Thus, persons subject to compulsory powers in the community under the Mental Health Act (i.e. those on Section 17 leave, conditionally discharged patients subject to Home Office restrictions and patients subject to Guardianship and Supervised Discharge) will not be entitled to the new payment.

The draft policy guidance suggests that offering direct payments in lieu of services to such patients would not guarantee the services being obtained. Whatever the justification, these patients may be disadvantaged. The Commission's view is that it is unnecessary to single out this group for blanket exclusion, as the Guidance also indicates that Local Authorities may set conditions to ensure the person's assessed needs are being met and that the money is being spent appropriately.

8.7   Supervised Discharge

Supervised Discharge was introduced in April 1996 and may prove helpful in the management of patients who, having recovered sufficiently to be discharged from hospital, are prone to refusing medication and other services and consequently are liable to relapse, with possible disastrous consequences to self or others. Treatment cannot be enforced, but contact with professionals is mandatory, allowing signs of deterioration to be detected early and readmission to hospital considered.

The Commission welcomes the recommendation of the recent Inquiry into the Care and Treatment of Martin Mursell (Crawford et al, 1997) that the remit of the Commission should be extended to cover Supervised Discharge, as was proposed by the Commission itself before the legislation was introduced. Currently, almost nothing is known about the effectiveness or otherwise of the use of the power. Although research has been commissioned by the Department of Health, an opportunity is being lost to monitor the operation of the power and evaluate the benefits and difficulties to the patients concerned, the services involved and the wider community. However, the Commission does have some involvement since the procedures leading up to the use of Supervised Discharge take place while detained patients are in hospital.

> **Heathlands Mental Health NHS Trust. Visit 17.3.97**
>
> Commission members examined a sample of statutory documentation relating to the 13 patients who were subject to Supervised Discharge at the time of the Visit. Each case was found to be extensively documented and the legal documentation was generally in order. In one case, however, a requirement to take medication was listed, even though this is not a legally enforceable condition.

The number of patients subject to Supervised Discharge at the Heathlands Mental Health NHS Trust is unusually high. Official statistics on the use of Supervised Discharge are not yet available, but Commission experience indicates that it has not been used for many patients, typically, just one or two by any one Trust. Furthermore, joint protocols, as recommended in the annex to the Code of Practice, have not been introduced everywhere. Prerequisites for an appropriate and positive use of Supervised Discharge are full implementation of the Care Programme

Approach (or the Welsh Mental Illness Strategy) and effective arrangements for Section 117 after-care.

8.8 Guardianship

Contrary to expectations, following the 1983 Act, Guardianship has been sparingly used. In many places, Guardianship has been viewed negatively; common criticisms being the limited powers of enforcement, the lack of a power to convey and the resource implications for Social Services Departments. However, its use is increasing and between 1985 and 1995 the number of Guardianship cases in England (in force at the end of the year) rose from 200 to 564. Over the same period, the number of new cases more than trebled from 97 to 372 (Dept. of Health, 1995b).

The principal target groups for Guardianship are people over the age of 65, particularly those suffering from dementia and those with learning disability. However, Guardianship has been used successfully for individuals with long term mental health problems. The Falling Shadow (Blom-Cooper, 1995), the Inquiry into the homicide of Andrew Robinson, a young man with a diagnosis of schizophrenia, reported how Guardianship proved to be successful in providing an appropriate framework of care whilst the order remained in force.

It might have been expected that the availability of Supervised Discharge would have reduced the use of Guardianship even further. On the contrary, there have been reports of more consideration being given to its use since the introduction of Supervised Discharge. This may have been triggered by discussion of the benefits of the three essential powers common to both: to determine residence, to require attendance for treatment and to have access to the patient by professionals.

Chapter 9

The Commission in Wales

9.1 Structural Changes

Statutory agencies involved in health and social care in Wales have experienced much structural change in the past two years. As of 1st April 1996, there are 5 Health Authorities (where previously there were 9) and 22 Social Services Departments (previously 8).

The change in visiting arrangements, including the introduction of the category of 'visiting' member and the new style Patient Focused Visits, has enabled more time to be spent in units with detained patients. The number of Visits to Trusts has increased, from one to two per year, with a joint Trust and Social Services Visit biennially. The creation of additional Social Services Departments has called for particular attention in the pre-Visit arrangements to ensure that all relevant Social Services Departments are involved in the biennial Visit.

9.2 Visiting Activity

From July 1995 to March 1997 a total of 13 full Visits and 35 Patient Focused Visits took place. For the first time, particular attention was paid to identifying all the Mental Nursing Homes in the area registered to take detained patients, of which 8 have been visited during this period.

Visits to forensic units continue, with Caswell Clinic, a Medium Secure Unit at Bridgend, visited on three and Llanarth Court, a private specialist unit in Monmouth, on six occasions. The latter included a Targeted Visit, which allowed for the examination of issues that had not been covered during Patient Focused Visits when most of the time was taken up with interviews. The topics raised on this Visit included content and recording of treatment plans, staff numbers and training, Managers' Reviews of detention, complaints procedure, medical cover and social work input. This proved a helpful exercise and it may be repeated elsewhere in Wales.

Meetings have been held with each of the 5 new Health Authorities to discuss issues relating to the Act and services for detained patients.

9.3   Extension of Forensic and Related Services

The Caswell Clinic has been extended to 35 beds, enabling the unit to provide more specialist facilities. At Llanarth Court, environmental changes to the two acute wards have provided additional space and an area for women only.

Plans to develop a Medium Secure Unit on the Bryn-y-Neuadd site on the North Wales coast were delayed because of the difficulty in the securing of capital, but approval has been given by the Welsh Office for it to be built and it is now scheduled to open in October 1998.

At present, it is the Commission's view that the Principality does not provide a good spectrum of care for people with difficult and/or challenging behaviour, that ranges from supported housing to some form of secure accommodation. This lack of facilities has led to some inappropriate placements as well as discharge delays.

9.4   Mental Health Act Issues

Formal admissions to NHS facilities in Wales have increased over the last four years, although there was a reported drop in 1993–94. There were 1300 admissions in 1995/96, over 50% more than the number reported in the late 1980s. The trends in the use of the Act show a similar pattern to those found in England (Welsh Office, 97) (see 3.1.1).

Supervised Discharge, Section 25, Mental Health (Patients in the Community Act, 1995), came into force in April 1996 (see 8.7) and Trusts, together with their Social Services colleagues have produced detailed policies, procedures and protocols. The Commission is pleased to learn that the Welsh Office has made funding available to Trusts and Social Services for staff training.

Revised statutory forms, which were introduced in April 1996 (see 3.1.2) appear to have been put in place successfully and the completion and checking of legal documents relating to the Act continues, in the main, to be done well.

Accessibility of Section 12(2) Approved doctors and of *GPs, out of hours*, (see 3.5.2 and 3.5.3) remains a problem in Wales as elsewhere. Most Health Authorities, whose responsibility it is to see there are sufficient approved doctors available, do have long lists, but many on the lists are not regularly available, especially 'out of hours'. At Commission meetings with Health Authorities the need for regular reviews of these lists, taking account of availability, has been emphasised. The development of GP consortia to provide out of hours services has caused problems in obtaining a patient's GP when needed for assessments. There has been discussion with clinicians to avoid inappropriate use of Section 4.

Consent to Treatment procedures (Section 58) continue to cause concern. Commission members on Visits have noted a number of occasions when Form 38 has not been completed according to the guidance in the Code of Practice (16.12). These lapses include:

- the completion of Form 38, days after the three month period has lapsed;

- doctors' changes to prescription sheets, resulting in a mismatch with Form 38;

- very occasional instances where the Form is not signed by the patient's own RMO, which means that nursing staff who then administer medication, without proper authorization, are doing so illegally.

It is suggested each Trust write up their own local policy and procedure to address these problems, building in a monitoring function for senior managers.

Availability of Approved Social Workers has been monitored by the Commission since the introduction of the new Unitary Authorities throughout Wales in April 1996. To date it has not been made aware of any real problems of non-availability of ASWs.

Section 136, the police holding power, appears to be used satisfactorily in Wales, with most Trusts having rewritten their policies to reflect the new Health Authority boundaries and the appropriate Police Authorities.

There have been a couple of problems in Gwent where people have been taken to the police station under Section 136 and, due to their rather disruptive behaviour, have had to remain in a police cell for a day or more until an appropriate unit has been found or their behaviour improves. Clearly, this is most unsatisfactory (see example at 3.3).

Section 17 leave has been closely scrutinised during the last year, both for its use and how it is recorded. Commission members have observed that, at all the Trusts and at Llanarth Court, policies and procedures have been developed and compliance by clinicians has been good.

Recalls of patients absent without leave (see 3.4) are affected by the 1995 Act, but Commission members have noted during visits that not all Trusts have rewritten their policies to reflect the new time scales.

Section 5(2) (see 3.2) seems to have been used more frequently by all Trusts. Whilst there is no obvious reason for this, a number of factors may contribute. These could include:

• patients being persuaded to be admitted informally and then wanting to leave;

• patients being unsettled because of patient mix and disruptiveness in acute wards;

• the reduction in de facto detention in Wales, where acute wards are not being locked and Section 5(2) is employed to keep patients in hospital.

Many Trusts have conducted detailed audits of the use of Section 5(2) during this period which show fewer Sections 5(2) being allowed to lapse without an assessment having been recorded.

Section 117 Aftercare policies and procedures have been well developed by all Trusts and Social Services. However, Commission members have noted from patients' records and from being informed by ASWs that there are still occasions when Section 117 meetings are called hurriedly or sometimes called spontaneously at a consultant psychiatrist's ward round. This means that persons are absent who should be involved in the detailed aftercare planning. One main reason given for this is the occasional need to discharge patients sooner than had been planned due to the pressure on beds and the need to admit more urgent cases.

9.5 Welsh Language Publications

The Welsh Language Act 1993 requires bodies which provide services to the public in Wales to provide a Welsh language facility. To assist in this matter the Commission has, upon request from Gwynedd Trust and Social Services Department, provided them with a Welsh language Report of its Full Visit, in addition to the English language Report. This is to be extended to all Trusts and Social Services Departments in Wales who will receive Full Visit Reports written in both languages upon request.

Currently, the Commission, the Welsh Language Board and the Welsh Office are in discussion about translation facilities and costs, not only for bilingual reports of Full Visits Reports but also for bilingual Patient Focused Visit Reports, Commission leaflets, Guidance Notes and other Commission publications.

It is intended that the Welsh Office will issue a Welsh language copy of the third revised Code of Practice when it is published.

During visits in the last year Commission members have been asked about availability of Mental Health Act legal forms in Welsh. Trusts have been advised to make representations to the Welsh Office. The Department of Health is liaising with the Welsh Office about this.

9.6 Hospital Closure

During this reporting period two mental illness hospitals have closed. The North Wales Hospital, in Denbigh, has been replaced by two smaller units providing services for Adults and Elderly Mentally Ill, in Wrexham and Bodelwyddan, together with enhanced community services. These two units are purpose built and offer a very high standard of accommodation and facilities. The Pen-y-Fal Hospital in Abergavenny, Gwent, closed in the Summer of 1996, as part of an overall plan aimed at decentralising services to make them more local and accessible. To support the reprovision of treatment, previously provided at Pen-y-Fal, hospitals have been developed at Ebbw Vale and Talygarn in Torfaen. These provide a wide range of services. Community Mental Health Teams continue to develop in the Gwent area.

Following closures of hospitals for people with learning disability, many patients have been discharged to small houses, flats and bungalows offering a very high standard of accommodation and service.

The Commission has been disappointed to learn of the delayed closure of Bryn-y-Neuadd Hospital in North Wales. However, efforts are being made to agree proposals and resettlement may begin within the next year.

9.7 Future Issues

Over the next two years, Commission members in Wales will be monitoring a number of areas of concern when visiting Trusts and Social Services Departments:

- bed occupancy in acute wards;
- services for women in hospital;
- the increase in acute admissions of patients with drug and alcohol problems.

Pennod 9

Y Comisiwn Yng Nghymru

9.1 Newidiadau Strwythurol

Y mae'r asiantaethau statudol sy'n ymwneud â iechyd a gofal cymdeithasol yng Nghymru wedi bod yn destun llawer o newidiadau strwythurol yn ystod y ddwy flynedd diwethaf. O Ebrill 1af 1996 ymlaen, y mae 5 Awdurdod Iechyd (ble yr oedd 9 cyn hynny) a 22 o Adrannau Gwasanaethau Cymdeithasol (8 cyn hynny).

Y mae'r newidiadau yn y trefniadau ymweld, gan gynnwys cyflwyno categori aelod 'Ymweld' a'r Ymweliadau 'claf-ganolog' newydd, wedi ei gwneud yn bosibl treulio rhagor o amser mewn unedau sydd â chleifion dan orchymyn. Y mae nifer yr Ymweliadau ag Ymddiriedolaethau wedi cynyddu, o un i ddau bob blwyddyn, gydag Ymweliad Ymddiriedolaeth a Gwasanaethau Cymdeithasol ar y cyd bob dwy flynedd. Y mae creu Adrannau Gwasanaethau Cymdeithasol ychwanegol wedi galw am sylw arbennig yn y trefniadau cyn Ymweld i sicrhau bod yr holl Adrannau Gwasanaethau Cymdeithasol perthnasol yn cymeryd rhan yn yr Ymweliad dwyflynyddol.

9.2 Gweithgaredd Ymweld

O Orffennaf 1995 hyd Fawrth 1997 fe gynhaliwyd cyfanswm o 13 Ymweliad llawn a 35 Ymweliad claf-ganolog. Am y tro cyntaf, fe dalwyd sylw arbennig i nodi'r holl gartrefi ymgeledd iechyd meddwl yn yr ardal a gofrestrwyd i dderbyn cleifion dan orchymyn, ac o'r cyfryw fe ymwelwyd ag 8 yn ystod y cyfnod hwn.

Y mae ymweliadau ag unedau fforensig yn parhau, gydag ymweliadau â Chlinig Caswell, Uned Ddiogelwch Ganolig ym Mhen-y-Bont ar Ogwr a dri achlysur a Chwrt Llanarth, uned arbenigol ym Mynwy, ar chwe achlysur. Yr oedd yr olaf yn cynnwys ymweliad darged, a oedd yn caniatáu archwilio materion nad oeddynt wedi eu cynnwys yn yr ymweliadau claf-ganolog pan dreuliwyd y rhan fwyaf o'r amser gyda chyfweliadau. Yr oedd y pynciau a godwyd ar yr Ymweliad yn cynnwys cofnodi cynlluniau triniaeth, niferoedd staff a hyfforddiant, Adolygiadau Rheolwyr ar gadwad, gweithdrefn gwyno, y trefniadau cyflenwol meddygol a chyfraniad gwaith cymdeithasol. Yr oedd hyn yn ymarferiad defnyddiol ac y mae'n bosibl y byddir yn ei ailadrodd mewn man arall yng Nghymru.

Fe gynhaliwyd cyfarfodydd gyda phob un o'r 5 Awdurdod Iechyd newydd i drafod materion sy'n ymwneud â'r Ddeddf a gwasanaethau ar gyfer cleifion dan orchymyn.

9.3 Ymestyniad ar Waith Fforensig a Gwasanaethau Perthnasol

Cafodd Clinig Caswell ei ymestyn i 35 gwely, gan alluogi'r Uned i ddarparu mwy o gyfleusterau arbenigol. Yng Nghwrt Llanarth, y mae newidiadau amgylcheddol i'r ddwy ward achosion difrifol wedi rhoi gofod ychwanegol ac ardal ar gyfer merched yn unig.

Y mae'r cynlluniau ar gyfer datblygu Uned Ddiogelwch Ganolig ar safle Bryn-y-Neuadd ar arfordir Gogledd Cymru wedi eu hoedi oherwydd yr anhawster i sicrhau cyfalaf, ond fe gymeradwyodd y Swyddfa Gymreig ei hadeiladu ac y mae bellach wedi ei harfaethu i agor yn Hydref 1998.

Ar hyn o bryd, barn y Comisiwn yw nad yw'r dywysogaeth yn darparu sbectrwm da o ofal ar gyfer pobl gydag ymddygiad anodd a/neu herfeiddiol, sy'n rhychwantu cartrefi cynalicdig hyd at ryw ffurf ar lety diogel. Y mae'r diffyg adnoddau yma wedi arwain at rai lleoliadau amhriodol yn ogystal ag oediadau ar ryddhau.

9.4 Materion y Ddeddf Iechyd Meddwl

Y mae'r Derbyniadau ffurfiol i gyfleusterau GIC yng Nghymru wedi cynyddu dros y pedair blynedd olaf er i ostyngiad gael ei gofnodi ym 1993-94. Yr oedd 1300 o dderbyniadau ym 1995/96, dros 50% yn fwy na'r nifer a gofnodwyd yn niwedd y 1980au. Y mae'r tueddiadau yn y defnydd a wneir o'r Ddeddf yn debyg o ran patrwm i'r rhai a ganfyddir yn Lloegr (Swyddfa Gymreig,97) (gweler 3.1.1)

Daeth Rhyddhau dan Oruchwyliaeth, Adran 25 Deddf Iechyd Meddwl (Cleifion yn y Gymuned,1995) i rym yn Ebrill 1996 (gweler 8.7) ac y mae'r Ymddiriedolaethau ynghyd â'u cyd-weithwyr yn y Gwasanaethau Cymdeithasol wedi cynhyrchu polisÿau, gweithdrefnau a phrotocol manwl. Y mae'r Comisiwn yn falch o ddeall bod y Swyddfa Gymreig wedi gwneud arian ar gael i Ymddiriedolaethau a'r Gwasanaethau Cymdeithasol ar gyfer hyfforddiant staff.

Y mae'r Ffurflenni Statudol Diwygiedig, a gawsant eu cyflwyno yn Ebrill 1996 (gweler 3.1.2) yn ymddangos fel eu bod wedi eu rhoi yn eu lle'n llwyddiannus ac y mae'r gwirio ar ddogfennau cyfreithiol sy'n ymwneud â'r Ddeddf yn parhau, ar y cyfan, i gael ei wneud yn dda.

Y mae Hygyrchedd at feddygon Awdurdodedig Adran 12(2) ac o Feddygon Teulu, y tu hwnt i oriau gwaith, (gweler 3.5.2 a 3.5.3) yn parhau i fod yn broblem yng Nghymru fel y mae mewn mannau eraill. Y mae'r rhan fwyaf o'r Awdurdodau Iechyd, cyfrifoldeb y cyfryw yw gweld bod digon o feddygon Awdurdodedig ar gael, gyda rhestrau meithion, ond nid yw llawer o'r rhai sydd ar y rhestrau ar gael yn rheolaidd, yn enwedig y tu hwnt i oriau gwaith. Mewn cyfarfodydd o'r Comisiwn gyda'r Awdurdodau Iechyd fe bwysleisiwyd yr angen am adolygiadau rheolaidd ar y rhestrau hyn, gan ystyried argaeledd. Y mae datblygiad consortia Meddygon Teulu i ddarparu gwasanaethau y tu hwnt i oriau gwaith wedi achosi problemau mewn cael gafael ar Feddygon Teulu'r claf pan fydd eu hangen ar gyfer asesiadau. Fe fu trafodaethau gyda chlinigwyr er mwyn osgoi defnydd amhriodol o Adran 4.

Y mae Caniatâd i weithdrefnau Triniaeth (adran 58) yn parhau i achosi pryder. Y mae aelodau'r Comisiwn ar ymweliadau wedi nodi nifer o adegau pan nad yw Ffurflen 38 yn cael ei chwblhau yn unol â'r cyfarwyddyd yn y Côd Ymarfer (16.12). Y mae'r llithriadau hyn yn cynnwys:

- cwblhau Ffurflen 38, ddyddiau wedi i'r cyfnod tri mis ddod i ben

- newidiadau gan ddoctoriaid i daflenni presgripsiwn, gan ddeillio ar anghytundeb â Ffurflen 38.

- adegau yn achlysurol iawn pan nad arwyddir y ffurflen gan SMA (RMO) y claf,sy'n golygu bod y staff nyrsio sydd wedi hynny'n gweinyddu moddion, heb fod ag awdurdod priodol, yn gwneud hynny'n anghyfreithlon.

Fe awgrymir bod pob Ymddiriedolaeth yn ysgrifennu eu polisi a'u gwcithdrefnau lleol hwy eu hunain i ymdrin â'r materion hyn, gan adeiladu ynddo swyddogaeth fonitro ar gyfer uwch reolwyr.

Y mae Argaeledd Gweithwyr Cymdeithasol Awdurdodedig wedi ei fonitro gan y Comisiwn ers cyflwyno'r Awdurdodau Unedol newydd ledled Cymru yn Ebrill 1996. Hyd yma ni chafodd ei wneud yn ymwybodol o unrhyw broblemau gwirioneddol ynglyn â diffyg argaeledd GCA.

Y mae'n ymddangos bod Adran 136, pwer atal yr heddlu yn cael ei defnyddio'n foddhaol yng Nghymru, gyda'r rhan fwyaf o'r Ymddiriedolaethau wedi ail ysgrifennu eu polisïau i adlewyrchu ffiniau'r Awdurdodau Iechyd newydd a'r Awdurdodau Heddlu priodol.

Fe fu un neu ddwy o broblemau yng Ngwent ble yr aethpwyd â phobl i orsaf yr heddlu yn unol ag Adran 136 ac, oherwydd eu hymddygiad braidd yn anystywallt, wedi gorfod aros yn un o gelloedd yr heddlu am ddiwrnod neu fwy hyd nes bod uned briodol wedi ei chanfod neu eu hymddygiad wedi gwella. Yn amlwg y mae hyn yn dra anfoddhaol, (gweler enghraifft yn 3.3).

Archwiliwyd Adran 17 — Caniatâd yn ofalus yn ystod y flwyddyn ddiwethaf, y modd y'i defnyddir a'r modd y'i cofnodir. Y mae aelodau'r Comisiwn wedi nodi bod polisïau a gweithdrefnau wedi eu datblygu ym mhob un o'r Ymddiriedolaethau ac yng Nghwrt Llanarth, a bod cydymffurfiad y clinigwyr wedi bod yn dda.

Effeithir ar Alw'n ôl gleifion sy'n Absennol heb Ganiatâd (gweler 3.4) gan Ddeddf 1995, ond y mae aelodau'r Comisiwn wedi nodi yn ystod ymweliadau bod yr holl Ymddiriedolaethau wedi ail ysgrifennu eu polisïau i adlewyrchu'r amserlenni newydd.

Y mae'n ymddangos bod Adran 5(2) wedi cael ei defnyddio'n fwy aml gan yr holl Ymddiriedolaethau. Tra nad oes yr un rheswm amlwg dros hyn, gall bod nifer o ffactorau yn cyfrannu. Fe allai'r rhain gynnwys:

- cleifion yn cael eu perswadio i gael eu derbyn yn anffurfiol ac yna eisiau gadael;

- cleifion yn methu a setlo oherwydd y gymysgedd o gleifion a tharfiadau mewn wardiau achosion difrifol

- gostyngiad yn y Gorchymyn de facto yng Nghymru, ble nad yw wardiau achosion difrifol yn cael eu cloi ac y defnyddir Adran 5.2 i gadw cleifion yn yr ysbyty.

Y mae llawer o'r Ymddiriedolaethau wedi cynnal archwiliad manwl i'r defnydd a wneir o Adran 5(2) yn ystod y cyfnod hwn sy'n dangos bod llai o Adrannau 5(2) yn cael eu gadael i derfynu heb i asesiad gael ei nodi.

Y mae polisïau a gweithdrefnau Adran 117 Ôl-ofal wedi eu datblygu'n dda gan yr holl Ymddiriedolaethau a'r Gwasanaethau Cymdeithasol. Fodd bynnag, fe wêl aelodau'r Comisiwn o gofnodion y cleifion ac o gael gwybodaeth gan GCAau fod yn parhau i fod adegau pan y gelwir cyfarfodydd Adran 117 yn frysiog neu ambell waith eu galw'n fyrfyfyr yn ystod ymweliad yr arbenigwr seiciatryddol â wardiau. Y mae hyn yn golygu bod personau a ddylai fod yn ymwneud â'r cynllunio ôl-ofal manwl yn absennol. Un o'r prif resymau a roddir dros hyn yw'r angen ar achlysur i ryddhau claf ynghynt nag y bwriadwyd oherwydd y galw am welyau a'r angen i dderbyn achosion mewn dwys angen.

9.5 Cyhoeddiadau yn yr Iaith Gymraeg.

Y mae Deddf Yr Iaith Gymraeg 1993 yn ei gwneud yn ofynnol i gyrff sy'n darparu gwasanaethau i'r cyhoedd yng Nghymru i ddarparu cyfleuster yn yr iaith Gymraeg.

Er mwyn bod o gymorth yn y mater hwn y mae'r Comisiwn, yn dilyn cais gan Ymddiriedolaeth ac Adran Gwasanaethau Cymdeithasol Gwynedd, wedi darparu adroddiad yn yr iaith Gymraeg iddynt ar ei Ymweliad llawn, yn ychwanegol at yr adroddiad yn yr iaith Saesneg. Fe ymestynnir hyn i'r holl Ymddiriedolaethau ac Adrannau Gwasanaethau Cymdeithasol yng Nghymru a fydd yn derbyn adroddiadau Ymweliadau llawn yn y ddwy iaith os y gwnânt gais am hynny.

Ar hyn o bryd, y mae'r Comisiwn, Bwrdd yr Iaith Gymraeg a'r Swyddfa Gymreig mewn trafodaethau ynglyn â chyfleusterau cyfieithu a chostau, nid yn unig am adroddiadau Ymweliadau llawn ond hefyd am Adroddiadau Ymweliadau claf-ganolog, taflenni'r Comisiwn, Nodiadau Cyfarwyddyd a chyhoeddiadau eraill o eiddo'r Comisiwn.

Y mae'n fwriad i'r Swyddfa Gymreig ddosbarthu copi yn yr iaith Gymraeg o'r trydydd Côd Ymarfer diwygiedig pan gyhoeddir ef.

Yn ystod ymweliadau dros y flwyddyn ddiwethaf fe ofynnwyd i aelodau'r Comisiwn os oedd ffurflenni cyfreithiol y Ddeddf Iechyd Meddwl ar gael yn Gymraeg. Fe gynghorwyd yr Ymddiriedolaethau i wneud cynrychiolaethau i'r Swyddfa Gymreig. Y mae'r Adran Iechyd yn cyd-drafod gyda'r Swyddfa Gymreig ynglyn â hyn.

9.6   Cau Ysbytai

Yn ystod y cyfnod yma y mae dau ysbyty afiechyd meddwl wedi eu cau. Y mae Ysbyty Gogledd Cymru, yn Ninbych, wedi ei disodli gan ddwy uned lai sy'n darparu gwasanaethau i Oedolion a'r Henoed gyda Salwch Meddwl, yn Wrecsam a Bodelwyddan, ynghyd â gwasanaethau estynedig yn y gymuned. Y mae'r ddwy uned hon wedi eu hadeiladu i'r perwyl ac y maent yn cynnig llety a chyfleusterau o safon uchel. Y mae Ysbyty Pen-y-Fal yn Abergyfenni, Gwent wedi ei gau yn Haf 1996, fel rhan o'r cynllun cyffredinol i ddatganoli'r gwasanaethau er mwyn eu gwneud yn fwy lleol a hygyrch. Er mwyn cynnal yr ail ddarpariaeth triniaeth, a ddarparwyd cyn hynny ym Mhen-y-Fal, fe ddatblygwyd dau ysbyty yng Nglyn Ebwy a Thalygarn yn Nhrofaen. Y mae'r rhain yn darparu amrediad eang o wasanaethau. Y mae Timau Iechyd Meddwl yn y Gymuned yn parhau i ddatblygu yn ardal Gwent.

Yn dilyn cau ysbytai ar gyfer pobl sydd ag anabledd dysgu, y mae llawer o gleifion wedi eu rhyddhau i dai bychain, fflatiau a byngalos sy'n cynnig safon llety a gwasanaeth uchel iawn.

Fe gafodd y Comisiwn ei siomi o ddeall am yr oedi yng nghau Ysbyty Bryn-y-Neuadd yng Ngogledd Cymru. Fodd bynnag, fe wneir ymdrechion i gytuno ar gynigion ac fe all ail gartrefu ddechrau o fewn y flwyddyn nesaf.

9.7 Materion y Dyfodol

Dros y ddwy flynedd nesaf, fe fydd aelodau'r Comisiwn yng Nghymru'n monitro nifer o feysydd sy'n achosi pryder pan fyddant yn ymweld ag Ymddiriedolaethau ac ag Adrannau Gwasanaethau Cymdeithasol.

- deiliadaeth gwelyau mewn wardiau achosion difrifol;

- gwasanaethau i ferched mewn ysbytai;

- y cynnydd mewn derbyniadau cleifion achosion difrifol gyda phroblemau cyffuriau ag alcohol.

Chapter 10

Special Issues

Summary

Seclusion policies and procedures, record keeping and monitoring are important and a matter for particular attention by the Commission. Some of the recommendations in the Code of Practice are not always being followed. The use of alternatives to formal seclusion should be monitored.

Control and Discipline policies on such matters as substance abuse, harassment, personal relationships and rules to preserve order need to be in place, particularly in view of some lack of clarity about legal powers of enforcement. The application of physical restraint can involve risks and the Commission would welcome guidance from the NHS Executive on the choice of appropriate courses of training. Abandonment of seclusion should not mean excessive use of physical restraint.

Independent Advocacy services are considered by the Commission to be important. During their Visits Commission members will be looking to see what advocacy services are available or planned.

Race and Culture provision for patients from ethnic minority cultures is often basic, insensitive and piecemeal. The Commission has devised a phased programme of action. For the first phase, *three target areas have been identified as a focus during Visits; ethnic monitoring, interpreters and racial harassment.*

Women's Issues are to receive particular attention at future Commission Visits. Only a minority of wards have policies dealing specifically with women's safety. Features of the physical environment of particular importance to women, such as lockable bedroom doors, self-contained washing and toilet facilities or a suitable place for visiting children, are too often lacking, although some units have made great efforts to improve.

Money Issues are of great concern to many patients. Benefit regulations are complicated and this is an area where advocacy is especially needed. It would also be of help to both hospitals and patients if new Department of Health guidance could be issued on the management of patients' money.

Learning Disability. Many mentally impaired patients whose capacity to manage their affairs is doubtful are treated as informal patients, often in locked wards, where they are de facto detained, without benefit of the protection of the Mental Health Act. The placement of patients with a dual diagnosis of mental illness and impairment continues to cause problems. Discharges to local facilities of learning disability patients from High Security Hospitals are subject to long delays. Dependency on agency nurses because of staff shortages weighs especially heavily on patients with learning disability who need the support of familiar people.

Mentally Disordered Offenders. Despite the increase in medium secure beds, demand still exceeds provision and patients from varied sources—prison transfers, high security discharges, court orders and transfers of patients from less secure units—compete with each other on waiting lists. The difficulty in finding community placements prepared to accept patients with a forensic history, or finding places to accommodate patients requiring long-term care under conditions of less security, adds to the problem. In some areas Court liaison schemes increase the demand for beds. There are concerns about the possible effects on the service of the Crime (Sentences) Act 1997.

Services for Adolescents have expanded, but they are unevenly distributed. Many adolescent patients, especially when accommodated by the independent sector, are at long distances from home. There are still some instances where adolescents are placed in adult wards, which is unacceptable.

The Mental Health Act needs to be reviewed. The diversification of types of facilities in which mental health care is delivered has introduced some difficulties in the operation of the Act and the definition of a hospital now needs urgent clarification. The lack of provision in the Act enabling the removal of abusive 'nearest relatives' remains a serious problem.

10 Special Issues

10.1 Seclusion

10.1.1 Seclusion Defined

The sudden imposition of solitary confinement is a serious event for any patient and carries a potential for provoking fear, resentment, humiliation or distrust. The procedure is not regulated by statute and its use is not limited to detained patients, but the Code of Practice offers detailed guidance on when and how it should be used. The definition of seclusion in the Code (18.15) is "the supervised confinement of a patient alone in a room which may be locked for the protection of others from serious harm". It requires proper authorization, periodic observation, formal recording and monitoring and the use of a suitably equipped room. Patients left alone in a room that is normally used for seclusion, but not locked in, or patients locked in a room with others, are not regarded as secluded.

The Commission is concerned that some Trusts and independent service providers do not have sufficiently clear policies and procedures when staff decide that patients should, in some way, be removed from their peers. For example, 'time out' away from other patients should not mean placement in a seclusion room even if the door remains unlocked.

Where seclusion is used the following is required:

- the seclusion room must be safe and conform to minimum requirements, e.g. adjustable heating and ventilation, optimum observation of the patient with no blind spots, suitable or purpose-built furniture and a call system the patient can use;

- a clear, up-to-date and accessible policy and procedure for staff to follow;

- a full record of every episode of seclusion and the reasons for it in the clinical notes and cross-referenced to the corresponding entries in a seclusion record book, bound and with sequentially numbered pages;

- properly completed forms for recording observations and reviews and times of doctors' attendance;

- the collection, analysis and monitoring of seclusion data.

10.1.2 Seclusion Practices

The Commission's Hospital profile statistics for 1995/6 show that nearly one third of independent hospitals and Trusts (142) reported using seclusion at least on one occasion. In total, there were 5,223 episodes of seclusion involving 2450 patients. A number had used seclusion for long periods of time; there were 30 hospitals where patients had been secluded for over 24 hours. (For a review of seclusion in the High Security Hospitals, see p.92).

The recording and monitoring of the use of seclusion is an important task in which nurses play a key role (Morrison and Lehane 1996). The reasons for each occasion of use, the periodic observations and the nursing and medical reviews required by the Code of Practice (18.15-23) all need to be recorded. It is good practice to record when food, drink and medication are taken by the secluded patient. There should be a clear and detailed seclusion policy to facilitate monitoring of compliance.

Examples of poorly equipped seclusion rooms are found occasionally.

> **Highbury Hospital, Learning Disabilities Directorate, Nottingham Healthcare NHS Trust: Visit 27.11.96**
>
> Commission members found the seclusion room on Highvale Ward measured only 6´0" by 6´6" with no room for a mattress or any furniture. The existing seat was inadequate, the light was not adjustable and no call system for patients was fitted. There were no separate heating controls and the room was overheated at the time of the visit. The seclusion room on Denby Ward was not much bigger. It had no natural light, no way to cover the observation panel in the door, a sluice drain in the middle of the floor, no heating, a dimmer switch on the light was not working, no call system for patients and slot head screws used in the door and the ventilation grill. At the time of the Visit the room smelt of urine. It had been used on 43 occasions in the period 14.6.96 to 26.11.96. The Commission recommended that there was an urgent necessity to review both rooms in relation to the guidance given in the Code of Practice. At a more recent Visit on 21.2.97, Commission members heard of a planned review of all seclusion by the Learning Disabilities Directorate as well as building work to go ahead in 1997.

In contrast, many seclusion facilities attracted no serious criticism and some were thought to be well-constructed and comfortably equipped with purpose-built furniture and en-suite toilet facilities that could be opened when required.

Some hospitals appear to have difficulty in adhering strictly to the Code of Practice guidance, particularly the requirement that a doctor should "attend immediately" when seclusion is implemented. The Commission recommends that seclusion record forms should have a space for recording the time of the doctor's arrival.

The use of seclusion as a means of preventing self harm is contrary to the Code of Practice, but still occurs occasionally. Pressure of beds can impinge on the use of seclusion, for example when a 'difficult to manage' patient, waiting in an unsuitable placement for transfer to a more secure environment, is subject to repeated or prolonged seclusion.

Hospital in London: July / August 1996

Concerns were raised by a solicitor about a patient, detained under Section 37/41, who had been kept in seclusion for three weeks. The Commission followed this up by interviewing the patient and investigating the circumstances. The patient had been placed in seclusion because he could not be managed on the open ward. Attempts had been made to transfer him to a secure unit, but a place could not be found. A few days after the Commission's intervention, a transfer to a secure unit did take place. The Commission drew the attention of the NHS Regional Office at South Thames to the case, who then asked the Health Authority to set up a review. The review panel made a number of recommendations to improve seclusion policy and practice in the Trust concerned and the relationship between the Trust and the Regional Forensic Service.

As a result of a number of concerns arising from Visits, the Commission will make seclusion a matter requiring particular attention over the next year.

10.1.3 Confinement without Seclusion

It has been noted on Commission Visits that, where service providers report a diminishing use of seclusion, examination of their records sometimes reveals frequent resort to related strategies variously described as "removal from the environment", "enforced segregation", "open door seclusion", "de-stimulation" or "placed in quiet room". These may be thought not to require the documentation and monitoring set out in the Code of Practice for the use of seclusion, but the Commission recommends that procedures used as alternatives to seclusion should be carefully recorded, monitored and audited.

10.2 Control and Discipline

10.2.1 Staff Powers

Maintenance of orderly and civilised conduct and the control of dangerous or disruptive behaviour are essential in the interests of both patients and staff of mental health units. Informal patients can be asked for an undertaking to abide by the rules on pain of discharge. For those detained against their will, the position is more difficult if they are unable or unwilling to co-operate. The restrictions imposed and the methods used to enforce them inevitably give rise to some complaints.

The law is less than explicit about the powers of staff to make rules and punish infractions. In emergency situations of potential violence, common law principles such as self defence, necessity and preventing a breach of the peace can be relied upon. The Mental Health Act confers powers to detain and to enforce treatment solely for mental disorder. However, a House of Lords ruling in *Poutney v Griffiths* (1975. 2 *All E.R.*, 888) supported the notion of necessary discipline of a detained patient over and above purely therapeutic measures. That case concerned the enforced termination of a visit from relatives, but the limits of what is reasonable remain largely untested. The imposition of penalties that are not part of a patient's therapy is problematic. It might be argued that they follow from a duty of care and are in the patient's best interests. It would appear that staff do have some disciplinary powers over their patients over and above matters incidental to treatment, although treatment need is commonly, if not always convincingly argued as the justification. For example, the Ashworth Inquiry (Blom-Cooper et al, 1992) criticised the continued seclusion of Sean Walton after "showing no remorse" (following suspected homosexual misconduct) as being unjustified on grounds of treatment needs.

John Creighton (1995), who has researched the problem of discipline in mental hospitals, points out that staff feel obliged to put an artificial therapeutic construction on all disciplinary measures. Genevre Richardson (1995) urges formal recognition of the need for discipline and the production of a disciplinary code with which patients would be required to co-operate. Given the legal uncertainties, Commission members have difficulty providing advice. The Code of Practice is helpful about non-confrontational measures to forestall aggression, and about the limited circumstances which justify emergency restraint or seclusion, but it is silent on powers to impose house rules or to discipline the defiant or to enforce participation at workshops, in occupational therapy, in group meetings or exercise sessions, any or all of which may be arguably part of treatment.

Staff need to impose some order for the sake of preserving the rights and safety of all. Staff at High Security Hospitals, in particular, have to manage patients who resist advice or persuasion. Rules, however, should not be arbitrary or oppressive. Staff may need to invade privacy to ensure that a detained patient is still present. They may need to limit the amount and type of objects brought onto the ward.

Incidents of obscene or threatening language, assaults on patients or staff, abuse of alcohol or drugs and sexually inappropriate behaviour all have to be controlled. Many such incidents are breaches of the law for which a complaint to the police could, perhaps should, be made. However, except in grave cases, staff attempt to cope without calling upon the police who, in any event, may be reluctant to prosecute detained mental patients unless some serious injury has occurred or drug trafficking is involved. It is incumbent upon Trusts to keep statistics of untoward incidents to facilitate monitoring of all such events and to produce policies for dealing with them, so that both staff and patients have clear guidance. When incidents lead to complaints, it should be verifiable whether accepted policy has been followed correctly. Full records of untoward occurrences, both in nurses' notes and on incident forms, provide protection from challenge particularly if patients' assertions, even though disputed, are also on record.

Physical restraints and seclusion and the policies governing them are discussed elsewhere (see 10.1 & 10.2.3). Patients' access to money is also discussed (see 10.6), but restrictions should only be considered where there is evidence of money being used for drug abuse or other criminal purposes, though even then legal authority may be lacking.

Personal searches are sometimes necessary, for example, when knives or other potentially dangerous objects go missing or when illicit drugs are thought to have been introduced into a ward. The Code of Practice advises on the conduct of searches, which should be carried out with minimum force and by a staff member of the same sex. It does not discuss legal powers, but stresses the need for an operational policy on all disciplinary matters which should be checked by Trusts' legal advisers.

Policies must reflect the patient mix to which they apply; secure units, closed wards and open rehabilitation centres need differing rules. However, Commissioners reading the Trust policies presented to them have been struck by variations in the amount of detail covered and also in the differing degrees of control attempted at apparently similar units.

Behaviour modification regimes, which allocate privileges in return for conformity, are considered an established form of therapy rather than a disciplinary technique, but are not always viewed as such by the patients who find themselves on wards run on these principles. Behavioural regimes tailored to the individual's needs are more purely therapeutic than a points system of earning privileges that applies uniformly to all patients. The Code of Practice (19.1) advises that patients' basic comforts should not be curtailed and, in the case of non-consenting patients, a suitably qualified person not on the treatment team should be consulted about the treatment plan.

10.2.2 Substance Abuse

Increasing abuse of drugs or alcohol by patients, described in the Sixth Biennial Report (9.6), continues to concern staff (Thomas, 1995) who often bring it to the attention of Commission members. The role of drugs as direct causes of persisting psychosis is a matter of dispute, but there is no dispute about the significant and apparently increasing association between drug abuse and psychiatric disorder, especially schizophrenia. Some patients may take drugs to alleviate their symptoms. Clinical observations suggest that consumption of cannabis and other illegal substances, with unknown interactions with prescribed medication, can exacerbate symptoms or provoke relapse into acute phases of illness (Cantwell and Harrison, 1996). Patients with schizophrenia, particularly if they are young males, are vulnerable to drug dependency (Smith and Hucker, 1994). Besides helping those already affected, it is important to protect others from becoming involved. Hard evidence on the precise incidence of illicit drug habits among patients is lacking, although it is likely to be especially prevalent among forensic patients who have experience of imprisonment (Liebling and McKeown, 1995). Cannabis is by far the most frequently detected illegal drug.

Trusts are slowly developing policies on substance misuse. Many units have strict rules against the use or possession of alcohol or drugs on wards and suspected dealers are reported to the police. Even more than with other control issues, however, enforcement gives rise to unresolved questions of legal authority. The policing of illicit drugs can involve searches of patients and their belongings, compulsory drug testing and confinement of those suspected of using leave off the ward to acquire cannabis or other drugs. Visitors found bringing in alcohol or drugs may have to be excluded. Police and sniffer dogs are sometimes called in. All these measures impinge upon individual rights. Some units discharge informal patients who break their rules, but for detained patients this is not an option.

Identifying and coping with the conflation of drug dependence and mental illness presents a challenge to staff. The Aintree Hospitals NHS Trust has initiated an in-depth study of the special needs of substance abusers and how they may be assessed and managed (Frost, 1996). How far drug-dependent people should be treated separately from other psychiatric patients remains an open issue. Their needs are often long-term and working relationships with other agencies, notably drug treatment centres, must be developed. Achievement of effective control, without being too confrontational, calls for special training. Even high security prisons appear unable to eliminate illicit substances completely. The Commission and the Royal College of Psychiatrists both see an urgent need for central and strategic guidance. At the Ministerial Review held in July 1996, the Commission suggested the formation of a multi-disciplinary Working Group, under the auspices of the Department of Health, to produce guidelines for good and consistent professional practice nationally.

10.2.3 Safe Restraint

The Commission is concerned about the number of incidents in which patients express resentment at what they consider to be the use of painful and unnecessary force, or are said to have sustained injury, sometimes severe, during attempts at physical restraint.

> In December 1994 an inquest heard how a detained patient had been restrained by four nurses for 45 minutes, while under medication, and had died soon afterwards. The staff had been trained in Control and Restraint methods, but a Home Office pathologist said in evidence that American research revealed a number of deaths following periods of Control and Restraint.

> On a Commission Visit to the Eric Shepherd Unit, Horizon NHS Trust, a patient was complaining about a second restraint injury incurred on 8 February, 1996 to an arm already fractured in an earlier episode of restraint.

The Commission supports the views on restraint put forward by the Royal College of Psychiatrists (1995a), particularly in its concern about inappropriate use of techniques of control through pain.

One of the dangers associated with restraint is that, following violent activity, the rate of absorption of anti-psychotic medication given by intra-muscular injection is greatly increased (Thompson, 1994). In February 1997, an inquest was informed that a patient had died seconds after being left in a seclusion room after a period of restraint. This patient had received large amounts of anti-depressant medication and had been given near maximum doses of anti-psychotic drugs by intra-muscular injection.

Despite advice of the Code of Practice (18.9), it appears that physical restraint is being used with increasing frequency. Reduction in the use of seclusion should not be at the cost of more frequent use of restraint and especially not prolonged episodes of restraint, which are particularly unpleasant for staff and patient and also potentially injurious.

St. Charles Hospital, Parkside NHS Trust: Visit 8.11.96

The use of seclusion had been discontinued. However, Commission members were concerned to note that a patient had been restrained by nurses for as long as one and a half hours. They felt this might have been avoided given the availability of alternative procedures and facilities for managing difficult behaviour.

The Commission commends the good practice of some units where the circumstances and timing and after-effects of episodes of restraint are systematically recorded in similar detail to episodes of seclusion.

Training for staff in safe methods of restraint is essential, but no officially endorsed Home Office or Department of Health training course, qualification or instruction manual exists. Most nursing staff receive training in Control and Restraint based on Home Office procedures within the High Security Hospitals, often from local staff who have been accredited as instructors by the High Security Hospitals. Ashworth Hospital, for example, has one of the better known systems. In the absence of an 'authorized' system there has been a rapid growth of alternative courses offering training for staff in a variety of settings where problems of aggressive behaviour can arise. Many units, particularly those operating degrees of security, have developed in-house techniques to meet their particular needs. Caswell Clinic in Gwent has developed a range of courses in the management of violence.

Some control systems, including the one developed at Ashworth (1996), have adopted the title 'Care and Responsibility'. This serves to emphasise that physical restraint is a last resort when skill in anticipation, negotiation and de-escalation of anger do not suffice to control a violent situation. The contexts in which violence may occur need to be recognised. Training in empathy and counselling and the development of understanding of why people behave violently are as relevant as techniques of physical restraint.

The lack of consistency of approach leaves staff vulnerable in the face of difficult situations. The Commission would welcome an initiative by the NHS Executive to audit current training and produce clearer guidance on those courses which offer the most appropriate training.

10.2.4 Relationship Policies

The control of emotional and sexual relationships is a controversial area. The goal of rehabilitation requires some freedom to pursue normal activities, but sexual activity creates special difficulty. An absolute ban on sexual contact with staff or on behaviour that amounts to a legal offence (sexual assault, harassment, public indecency, indecent exposure) is unchallengeable, but a total ban on all consensual heterosexual (or for that matter homosexual) behaviour, especially for long-stay patients, is more question-able.

Restrictions are, however, sometimes part of the duty of care. For example, a patient's husband or other relatives, as well as the patient herself, might well complain if, while disinhibited through illness, she were to be exposed to risk of pregnancy or sexual infection.

Trust policies adopt different approaches. Some state categorically that sexual intercourse on the premises is forbidden. For short-stay patients and those granted Section 17 leave this may not create problems. Where a more permissive policy is in place, considerations of privacy, contraception and sexual counselling arise. Long-term detained patients are not legally precluded from marrying and some marriages have taken place with approval and support from clinicians.

A clear policy on sexual relationships, suited to the unit and its patients, provides a necessary support to staff in dealing with the dilemmas that can arise.

10.3 Advocacy Services for Detained Patients

The Commission supports the provision of an independent advocacy service available to detained patients to help them secure for themselves due attention to their needs, interests and rights. The importance of this has been highlighted in the booklet, *The Patient's Charter and Mental Health Services* (Dept. of Health, 1997b). The Charter states that patients can expect to be told about any local advocacy schemes or support groups for people who use mental health services and that they can expect to have a relative, friend or other person of their choice support them or speak or act on their behalf. The Commission appreciates the heavy demands on hospital resources, but considers advocacy, and staff training in its use, to be important. During Visits Commission members will be looking to see what advocacy services are available or planned.

Mental health workers cannot be independent advocates themselves for clients of their services, although they can perform an advocacy function at times. There are differences between the views of professionals, users and carers as to what are the important issues. Studies have shown that users are likely to highlight housing, friend-ship and personal support, whereas professionals tend to emphasise treatments, moni-toring of symptoms and the importance of services provided by professional organisations (Shepherd, G. et al., 1994)

Independent advocacy can be provided by various outside agencies and in a number of different forms, but it should always have the same aim, that is to enable patients to express views about any aspect of their care and treatment without fear of detrimental consequences. Advocates can help support patients in decision-making and personal planning, especially when in contact with professionals on ward rounds and on other occasions.

One form of advocacy, akin to the legal model, is where independent advocates, paid or voluntary, support individual patients when they have a problem concerning, for example, rights under the Mental Health Act or access to services or welfare benefits. They can also help patients to put forward their views at Hospital Managers' Hearings, to make better use of reviews and complaints procedures and to obtain legal advice and representation where appropriate. There is a great demand for this type of advocacy and its value is acknowledged by the majority of hospitals, but more could be done to promote the development of services. In some areas the Citizens Advice Bureau and other voluntary organisations such as MIND are given limited funding to provide a service.

Another form of advocacy, the Patients' Councils and Patient Council Support Groups, is provided by people with experience as users of mental health services. They can help to bring concerns to the attention of management. Patients' Councils have been set up in a number of areas, including Nottingham, Bristol, Powys, Liverpool and Shropshire (Holmes, G. 1996) and they are also established in the High Security Hospitals.

One example of good practice, brought to the attention of the Commission is in Nottingham, where an agreement has been negotiated between Nottingham Advocacy Group and Nottingham Healthcare Trust, which acknowledges the status of the Patients' Council and facilitates access of advocates to patients, with their consent. However, elsewhere, Patients' Councils are not always encouraged and funding difficulties have prevented many units from starting or maintaining such a service. In the South West a Patients' Council was established which was highly valued by patients for the help given them in stating their views at ward rounds and assessments, but it has not been continued. At another hospital in the same Region, money was spent recruiting and training volunteers to meet a demonstrated need for independent advocacy, but further funding has not been forthcoming and the service is unlikely to become available to patients unless a lottery bid proves successful.

10.3.1 Advocacy for Patients with Learning Disability

Patients with learning disability have an obvious need for advocacy, but the Commission finds little provision for it in hospital or available from community based schemes. Advocacy is particularly needed by patients who are being resettled and who have to make decisions about accommodation and future care. CAIT (Citizen Advocacy Information and Training) in London can supply information about existing advocacy schemes or the availability of advocates. 'Citizen Advocacy', based in Sutton, Surrey, has a long established scheme, providing advocates for people with learning disability both in hospital and the community.

10.4 Race and Culture

10.4.1 The Range of Issues

Provision for patients from ethnic minority communities often remains basic, insensitive and piecemeal, leading to patients feeling alienated and isolated. It is dispiriting that the serious issues of inappropriate care and treatment of patients from black and ethnic minority communities, which were raised in previous Biennial Reports, continue to cause concern and to be noted in reports of Commission Visits.

The Commission has an ongoing commitment to address inequalities, not only when carrying out Visits and interviewing detained patients, but also within its internal organisation, for example in the recruitment and training of Commission members and in the support given to the implementation of its Equal Opportunities and Race and Culture policies. The Commission has recently revised its Visiting Policy to highlight the importance of race and culture issues and issued Guidelines indicating the relevant questions to raise with staff and patients. Commission members need to be pro-active in interviews with patients who may be diffident about raising such issues on their own initiative.

Matters relating to black and ethnic minority patients of concern to the Commission include the following.

i **Care.** How are the patients' particular requirements being met in respect to diet, hair and skin care, religious observances, suitable activities and health needs?

ii **Training.** Does training for staff include racism awareness, anti-discrimination practice and understanding of the possible effects of stereotyping on diagnosis and estimations of dangerousness? Is there support and supervision for staff on these issues?

iii **Interpreters.** Do patients have access to trained, independent interpreters speaking their own language or dialect and available when needed?

iv **Information.** Are patients given access to local organisations, advocacy projects and religious groups from their own ethnic community? Are staff aware of and in touch with the available facilities?

v **Policies.** Does the hospital/unit have policies on ethnic matters, including racial harassment policies and staff recruitment? Is there adequate monitoring of the implementation of policies? Have changes been made by purchasers or providers as a result of ethnic monitoring?

The Commission includes a number of members with particular expertise and experience in race and culture matters. It would be unrealistic, however, to expect all members to possess the skills, knowledge and experience to address each and every one of the issues involved. Therefore, through its Quality Standards Group, the Commission has devised a phased programme of action. For the first phase, three target areas have been identified as a focus during Visits, namely ethnic monitoring, interpreters and racial harassment. All Commission members will be given the training to deal with these issues.

10.4.2 Ethnic Monitoring

Britain has a multi-racial, multi-ethnic society, with 6.2% of the population belonging to a different ethnic group from the majority, white population. There is growing awareness that people with differing racial and cultural backgrounds display different disease patterns and have different health service needs. Various reports have found that black and ethnic minority people are less likely to find health services which are adequate, appropriate and accessible.

Lack of ethnic monitoring is one of the important reasons for an absence of data on the health status of certain minority ethnic groups. An NHS Executive Letter (1994) came into operation on April 1st 1995, making ethnic monitoring mandatory for all NHS hospital in-patients, but compliance began very slowly in some hospitals. Consequently, there are no comprehensive national figures for 1995/96. During Visits, Commission members have found ethnic monitoring very patchy and ad hoc, with some facilities ignoring the requirement.

Ethnic monitoring has many purposes, including the following:

- to determine current service usage

- to identify gaps in the service

- to assess health needs of the minority ethnic communities

- to improve quality of services

- to evaluate changes in services

- to achieve equal access to services

- to provide a baseline for planning

- to measure health improvements.

Ethnic monitoring can provide a more accurate picture than is otherwise available of the current use of services by people from various communities. It can raise questions that warrant further examination and it can provide a baseline for planning, target setting, measuring change and ultimately measuring health outcomes.

As a matter of course on Visits, Commission members check that ethnicity has been recorded on the patients' files on the ward and that the Census categorisation is being used. Ethnic monitoring by the Commission of requests for Second Opinions is already in place (see 5.2).

10.4.3 Interpreters

The availability, training and use of interpreters has been a long-standing concern. Reports from Commission Visits continue to suggest that this remains a low priority for service providers. Problems range from lack of staff training in the use of interpreters to the bad practice of using cleaning staff, relatives or even other patients as interpreters. Trained and qualified interpreters are often unavailable, but when they are available they are not always used to the best advantage; they may not be called upon for ward rounds or on other occasions (e.g. SOAD or Commission Visits) when the patient needs them most.

Lack of a comprehensive interpreter service can lead to patients not having their rights properly explained to them, not receiving psychological treatments or being unable to communicate with their key nurse, all of which can increase anxiety and a sense of isolation.

10.4.4 Racial Harassment

During Commission Visits incidents of racial abuse between patients, and occasionally from staff to patients, have been noted. This is extremely damaging to recipients, worsening the sense of isolation that many may be feeling already. On occasion, a victim of abuse has been goaded into hitting out physically and has then been placed in seclusion. When such issues have been put to staff they have often not known how they should respond.

Where clear policies and procedures directed towards pertinent issues have not been developed, or are not readily to hand, staff cannot be expected to know exactly what steps to take if, for example, a black patient is being continually exposed to racial abuse.

The Commission hopes that senior management will take these issues more seriously and, by acknowledging and rectifying shortcomings in policy, training and practice, will improve conditions for black and ethnic minority patients. Progress in this regard cannot but be of benefit to other groups as well, women in particular.

10.5   Women's Issues

10.5.1 Introduction

There is a substantial body of evidence about differences in the origins and nature of mental disorder experienced by women and men and also about the ways in which they are treated. Women and men have different needs which demand different responses from service providers and the Commission.

10.5.2 Needs of Detained Women Patients

While women are in the majority among patients of most mental health units, this is no longer the case with detained patients. The proportion of women compulsorily detained under Part II of the Act has declined from 57% in 1987/8 to 49% in 1995/6. Just 12% of court disposals under the Act are for women and here again the percentage is declining (Dept. of Health, 1995a, 1997a). The proportion of women compared to men changes with age. Under the age of 35, more men are admitted. In older age groups, the balance changes and the proportion of women increases along with age. Nevertheless, at all ages the number of detained women remains substantial and policies specifically for them are essential.

The reasons for admission differ for women. Their ordinary life experiences impact on vulnerability to mental illness. Childbirth is linked to risk of depression. Caring for children and dependent relatives when associated with isolation, low social value and a lack of resources increases the risk of mental health breakdown. Cultural expectations concerning female body image may be part of the reason why anorexia nervosa occurs mainly in women.

There is now evidence that abnormal, but not unusual, experiences of abuse (physical, sexual and emotional) have serious consequences for women. Domestic violence, which can be linked to long-term mental health problems, is estimated to occur in 1 in 4 households, mostly inflicted on women by male partners. Many of the women receiving psychiatric services are found to have experienced sexual or physical abuse in childhood. A figure of 80% has been cited for women patients in High Security Hospitals.

Research has pointed to links between history of abuse and self harm and suicide attempts. For example, a study of 53 women patients at Ashworth High Security Hospital found only 3 without a history of self harm and 62% who were still self-harming.

10.5.3 The Service Response

Gender influences the way services respond to needs, including how assessments under the Act and decisions to admit under compulsion are made. Violent and aggressive behaviour is more likely to be regarded as abnormal when displayed by women. When behaviour is in need of control men are more likely to go to prison, women to a psychiatric hospital or secure unit. The role of women as carers may mean that their disturbed behaviour is likely to be seen as a threat to others in the family and lead to compulsory admission.

Safety for women on psychiatric wards is a major issue, especially where staffing levels are low and violence considerable, as in the London area. A patient mix including men with a history of violence and young women with a history of abuse occurs on some wards. It has been reported to the Commission that Approved Social Workers (ASWs) are having to take such risk factors into account when considering applying for an admission. Women are particularly vulnerable in Regional Secure Units where there may be very few other female patients and a lack of female staff.

Mother and baby units are sometimes unsuitably placed in a corner of an acute ward. Staff generally are not trained to care for babies and Health Visitors do not visit the wards.

The Patients' Charter standard, offering a choice of single sex accommodation, is rarely met. This is a particular need for women from ethnic minorities whose cultural and religious practice forbids contacts with men. Although many units have made considerable efforts to provide safe facilities for women and to preserve their privacy and dignity, there remains much room for improvement. The findings of the Commission's National Visit (1.8) show that just over a third (35%) of women have access to women-only sleeping areas (i.e. self-contained with exclusive bath/shower and toilet facilities); a quarter (27%) have to pass male parts of the ward to reach women-only toilets, bath or showers; a third (32%) have access only to mixed sex toilets, bath or shower facilities. A small number (3%) use sleeping areas also used by men.

Only a minority of units in the National Visit reported having policies dealing specifically with women's safety, although, when questioned, 58% of nurses thought there were issues of sexual harassment of women patients by male patients on the ward. One nurse saw "no problem", but recalled two sexual assaults the previous year! There is a need for staff to be continually alert to women's sexual vulnerability.

Some units are making great efforts to improve responsiveness to women's needs.

Homerton Hospital, City and Hackney Community Services NHS Trust: Visits 27/ 28.6.96 and 19.12.96
It was noted in the Hospital's response to the June visit that since April there had been 5 incidents of sexual harassment reported, ranging from suggestive comments to physical contact. At the subsequent visit it was evident that the hospital had taken positive action to

deal with the problem. Facilities for women were provided on all wards. Two female clinical psychologists had been appointed to link with two wards and to ameliorate concerns about the vulnerability of women. It was noted also that more women were being admitted and the provision of a women-only Intensive Care Unit was under consideration.

St.Clement's, Tower Hamlets NHS Healthcare Trust.

During a series of visits in 1995 the Commission reported its concern about women having to walk through a men's toilet area to get to the bathroom. On a Visit in February 1996 it was noted that one ward had been completely refurbished to a very high standard and separate dormitories for men and women had been created. A mother and baby unit had been installed and further work was planned to enhance the bathroom and toilet facilities. However, on a Visit in September following, the need for vigilance was noted, a man having been seen in the female dormitory.

Airedale General Hospital, Airedale Trust: Visit 16.9.96

The Commission was impressed with improvements on one ward where a women's lounge had been created with its own television, video and toilet facilities. Women could see their children and other visitors with a degree of privacy. The additional video was beneficial, because it afforded ethnic minority groups greater opportunity to watch videos in their own language.

An adequate service for women should include staff training in women's needs, the provision of information about relevant support groups and advocacy services and attention to gender specific medical needs. There must be easy access to necessary sanitation protection and toiletries. Hairdressing and beautician services should be available. There should be mixed gender staff on all shifts and, when possible, patients should be able to choose a male or female key nurse. The availability of a woman psychiatrist may be of particular significance to some women, especially those from some ethnic minority cultures. The production of a clearly defined, implemented and audited policy for the care and safety of women patients is of great importance.

10.5.4 The Commission Response

The Commission is reviewing its own performance regarding women's issues. Women patients are under-represented at interviews with Commission members (see 2.2). It is also evident that issues related to women are not being routinely identified, since they are mentioned in only 22% of Visit reports, of which 30% identify services as being below acceptable standard.

Women's issues was one of the themes of the National Visit, which provided extensive information on current services for women. Women's care has also been selected as a "matter requiring particular attention" on Commission Visits, which will involve systematic monitoring of selected items about staffing and facilities for women.

The Quality Standards Group, an internal Commission planning group, has been given the task of reviewing and improving Commission activity by updating existing internal guidance. This includes a checklist on women's issues and the training of Commission members in its use and in their awareness of the relevant issues. The aim is to ensure that the right questions are asked during all Visits, so that information is elicited in a form to help purchasers and providers to identify deficiencies and promote good practice in their services for detained women patients.

10.6 Money Issues

10.6.1 Introduction

Money issues can add to the stress of detention in hospital and are increasingly being raised on Commission Visits. Patients' concerns are about benefits in general and about detailed changes in benefit regulations. Issues also arise about the management of patients' money, the power of hospital managers or consultants to withhold access to it and arrangements for taking over control of patients' money and affairs. Neglect of money matters during a period of detention, besides heightening anxiety, can lead to serious problems of indebtedness, loss of housing and inadequate preparation for discharge. Some issues of special relevance to detained patients are outlined in the following paragraphs. A more detailed discussion can be found in a report edited by G. Zarb (1996).

10.6.2 The Benefit System

The benefit system responds in complex ways to changes in personal circumstances occasioned by hospital admission. Detained patients experience special problems because they tend to have repeated admissions or to remain in hospital long enough for entitlement to benefits to change. They may also be allowed periods of leave under Section 17, for which specific claims should be submitted. The Sixth Biennial Report (10.9) emphasised the importance of communication between the agencies involved (the hospital, the Benefits Agency, the housing authority and the patient's key worker) to ensure that the correct benefits are paid at the right time. Since that Report, significant changes in benefit regulations have occurred. One example is the *Mobility Component of Disability Living Allowance*, which, with effect from July 1996, has been aligned with the care component and ceases to be paid after 4 weeks stay in hospital. Transitional protection, offered to those who had been in hospital for

12 months when the regulations came into force, was not extended to (forensic) patients detained under Part III of the Act. Criticism of the payment of benefits to offenders had appeared in the press. Hospitals need to take account of the consequential loss of income for some patients.

Norvic Clinic, Norfolk Mental Health Care NHS Trust: Visit 10.10.96

Commission members noted that at the Highfield Hostel, where patients cater for themselves, following the reduction in Disability Living Allowance, patients were left with only £23 per week to cover food and cleaning materials plus approximately £12 for any additional needs and no provision for patients' travel costs for shopping trips and other visits outside the hospital. The Hospital Management was asked to consider whether they could compensate for the reduction in income by increasing the allowances paid to the patients. Patients had raised the issue because their activities were being limited.

10.6.3 Hospital Policies and Procedures on Money

Most hospitals have Patients' Affairs Officers responsible for receiving income paid to patients and issuing them with money for personal use. Department of Health guidance on this dates back to a Hospital Memorandum on Patients' Moneys (H.M. (71) 90), which has never been updated. Patients nowadays expect to have as much control as possible over their own affairs and the old guidance is no longer so relevant. There is considerable confusion amongst health professionals and administrators, as well as amongst patients and their relatives and carers, as to what arrangements can be made to take over patients' finances or when access to money can be lawfully denied. Patients are not always made properly aware of how to have access to their money and may be led to believe they have no right (or need) to ask for money. In fact, the law assumes that all adults are capable of looking after their own affairs without interference, whether or not they are in hospital, until the contrary is proved. Legal authority is required, for example from the Court of Protection, before anyone, whether a professional or family member, can take over the affairs of a person incapable of managing their own affairs. The powers of hospital managers or consultants to restrict detained patients' access to their money or control over their affairs are strictly limited to specific circumstances. Patients must be given information about how their money is being managed and should also have a right to challenge decisions made by the hospital to control their money.

Hospital in Midlands: Visit 1.3.96

A patient complained that her money was being withheld by nursing staff who gave her a small daily allowance. The Commission members advised that the RMO should be certain

---

the patient was not capable of controlling her own affairs by dint of mental illness, rather than merely being prone to use money unwisely. If it was intended to restrict money for any length of time, further legal authority would be necessary. In the absence of evidence that it is being used for unlawful purposes, there is no statutory authority to withhold money from patients who have the capacity to control their affairs. The money, in this case, was being used to buy alcohol and was contributing to the difficulty in the management of illicit drug use and alcohol use on the ward. The Commission advised in subsequent correspondence that there would be no difficulty if a patient gives proper and informed consent to restrictions on the access to their money. However, it also needs to be understood that such consent may be withdrawn at any time by the patient.

It would be of great benefit to both hospitals and patients, and particularly to psychiatric units, if new Department of Health guidance could be issued on these matters. Meanwhile, units should devise their own policies and procedures. They can refer to a booklet, *Other People's Money*, issued by Age Concern (1992). Hospitals should also ensure that they hold a stock of benefit leaflets and claim forms on display for patients. Providing information about welfare benefits should be viewed as part of the duty of Hospital Managers to give information to detained patients (see Jones, 1996 at 1–773). There is a need for expert help and advice on benefits to be available in hospitals and the Commission has observed that, where this exists, it is well used and valued by patients. ASWs also need to be clear about their responsibilities with regard to money and/or personal property. For example, they should ensure that arrangements are made to safeguard the home and belongings of detained patients after admission and that pets are being looked after.

10.6.4 Individual Care Plans

The Commission, in the Sixth Biennial Report (10.9), identified a need for income maintenance to be written into every patient's care plan. When checking Section 117 and related documentation, Commission members may note whether money issues are covered.

Plans should cover arrangements for patients to claim their entitlement while on Section 17 leave at home. There are particular complications because of the different benefit offices to which claims may have to be submitted. There may also be difficulties because any increase in benefit for periods of leave is paid in arrears, so that patients may have little money with which to support themselves during the time they are on leave at home. If patients on Section 17 leave return from home to hospital at night, they will still only receive hospital rate benefits, despite having to meet travel costs and support themselves in the community during the day. Care planning should also identify needs of informal carers or relatives for financial assistance to cover travel costs for visits to patients, especially when patients are accommodated at a distance on an extra contractual referral basis.

10.6.5 Forensic Patients' Entitlements

There are wide variations in benefit entitlements between patients detained under different sections of Part III of the Act. Prisoners transferred on Section 47/49 are not eligible for the same benefits as those detained under Section 37 or 37/41 (court orders). The Sixth Biennial Report drew attention to this issue (7.4, p.77).

For benefit purposes patients classed as 'technical lifers' (i.e. transferred from prison to secure hospital in recognition that a Hospital Order might have been appropriate at the time of sentence) should be treated as if on Section 37. The same applies to 'notional 37s' (i.e. Section 47/49 transfers who have passed the expected date of release from prison). Benefits agencies, however, are inconsistent in their approach to these patients. Those on remand sections (35, 36, 38 and 48) are prisoners for benefit purposes, but if ultimately given a Hospital Order they may be eligible for back payment of sickness benefits for their remand period. Patients in secure environments are not generally able (for security reasons) to hold their own bank books, so daily financial transactions are dealt with on a requisition basis, via a hospital account. For administrative ease, the Benefits Agency have a scheduled bulk payment arrangement with hospitals, whereby the finance department of the hospital distributes the money. All of this makes it more difficult for patients to keep track of their entitlements.

10.7 Services for Patients with Learning Disability

10.7.1 Informal Patients

Only 254 patients classified as mentally impaired and 25 as severely mentally impaired were detained under the Act in the year ending 31 March 1995 (Dept. of Health 1996a), but this does not include those with a dual diagnosis who are categorised as 'mentally ill'.

The Commission continues to be concerned about people with learning disability who remain in hospital informally, but 'involuntarily'. The Commission is aware that inaccurate and ill-founded assumptions are often made about the incapacity of patients with learning disability to make decisions, including decisions about medical treatment, money matters and discharge from hospital. However, many of them will actually be able to make their own decisions and they should be consulted and enabled to take decisions whenever possible. The provision of an advocate to enable and support decision making is important, but rarely available.

Patients who lack capacity are rarely sectioned. Among this group are some who are described as having challenging or difficult behaviour. They are often treated with continuous and high doses of medication. If they have not been detained under the Act, the Commission does not have jurisdiction to interview them or to investigate complaints by them or made on their behalf. These patients have no statutory safeguards, no access to Mental Health Review Tribunals, no Second Opinion reviews of medication, no powers of the nearest relative to discharge and no contact with the Commission.

The Code of Practice (18.27) provides some guidance about safety and security for patients with learning disability who are informal, but who are considered at risk on the ward. For patients who "persistently and purposely attempt to leave a ward" it is recommended that detention under the Act should be considered.

For patients who are restrained or treated on locked wards all hospitals should have current 'locked door' policies and up-to-date treatment plans. The Commission is aware of hospitals where no such policies exist or are not known to ward staff. When informal patients are restrained or secured in hospital or in the community this is under common law principles. Staff, carers and patients should be aware of this and of the limits to practice under common law.

Patients with learning disability are often placed in small community units which the Commission may not often visit if they rarely accommodate detained patients. The Commission continues to recommend that its remit be extended to patients who are in hospital informally and who are unable to make some or all of their own decisions, many of whom are de facto detained.

The Commission in its Sixth Biennial Report (2.3) welcomed the Law Commission (1995) recommendations for reform of the law on decision making by and for adults who lack capacity and regrets that they have not been implemented.

10.7.2 Patients with Learning Disability and Mental Illness

The Commission is aware that there is no nationally agreed policy on the provision of psychiatric services for patients who have learning disability. Commission members have seen patients with learning disability whose mental illness has remained undiagnosed for periods of time while others were being treated inappropriately on acute admission wards with the mentally ill. Both these situations were problematic and some patients have been found to have waited a long time for appropriate admission and treatment. When there are changes in the classification of a detained patient, from mental illness to mental impairment, this indicates the need for a different placement with a learning disability service, but appropriate beds are not necessarily available. The Royal College of Psychiatrists (1995a) has pointed out the particular difficulties for the care of patients with learning disability caused by the divided responsibilities, in both community and hospital services, when impairment is complicated by problems of aggressive behaviour that may be due to mental illness. The Commission's experience indicates that local agreements for the provision of services for patients with a dual disorder are urgently needed.

10.7.3 Secure Provision

The Commission is concerned about the lack of provision for patients who need long-term medium secure care in hospital or continuing care in the community. Some patients with learning disability continue to be treated in High Security Hospitals, mainly at Rampton. All such patients should be subject to active discharge planning in conjunction with the responsible Local Authorities. The Commission is aware of patients waiting long periods for discharge who have lost touch with local services. In Rampton, some women with learning disability have been cared for on wards with patients who have mental illness. This is an issue for the High Security Psychiatric Services Commissioning Board to consider in its future strategy.

10.7.4 Care and Treatment in Hospital

The use of agency nursing staff, common in most hospitals, is particularly problematic for patients with learning disability who need a familiar and consistent staff group. They may have impaired capacity, poor communication and physical disabilities. In suggested changes to the revised Code of Practice, to be published in 1997, the Commission has stressed the importance of recognising and providing for physical disabilities, including visual and hearing impairments, as well as providing signing, Makaton and other communication aids. Commission members have found patients with severe mental impairment who have been poorly assessed or treated because of failure to communicate, absence of advocacy, lack of consultation with experts or with carers who have relevant information about them. The Commission will continue to look for the implementation of the recommendations of the Mansell Report for high quality, individualised provision of services for people with learning disability.

Many hospitals for patients with learning disability have closed during the period of this Report. The Commission reiterates the comment in its Sixth Biennial Report (7.3) about the many examples of good practice in the resettlement of hospitalised patients. However, there have also been examples of patients discharged to the community as part of a resettlement programme who have returned to hospital under a section because the community provision has failed to address and contain difficult behaviour.

The Commission will continue to monitor the quality of discharge planning for detained patients with learning disability and the application of the Code of Practice as it relates to them. The Commission is pleased to note that much good work and improvement is taking place.

Kingsbury Hospital, Parkside NHS Trust: Visit 8.11.96

Improvements were recorded in the recruitment of trained nurses, including the appointment of a nurse to do outreach work and community service. Funding had been provided for an increased psychology service. Commission members were impressed with the planning and recording arrangements for Section 117 and the improved attendance at multidisciplinary meetings that had been achieved.

On Kenton Ward, since the division of rooms, greater privacy had been achieved and the ward had been extended to include a rehabilitation area. On Carlton Ward, staff had made efforts to involve patients in redecorating.

The staff in charge of detained patients at small residential units away from a main hospital need to be familiar with the Act and keep a check on consent forms, and leave status.

Rockingham Forest NHS Trust: unannounced Visits 10.2.97, 27.2.97

Staff at two residential units were unfamiliar with the Act, whilst unqualified staff at 4, Kirby Close thought the Act did not apply to a Learning Disability Service. The staff member in charge at Willows (an assessment and treatment unit) had had no training on the Act since qualifying 11 years ago and the staff member in charge at 10 Westfield Road had had only one day of training in 1995.

The situation was made worse through shortages of qualified staff. At Willows, night duty was being done by unqualified staff. Doors were kept locked, although there were informal patients.

10.8. Mentally Disordered Offenders

10.8.1 Forensic Psychiatric Services

Since the publication in 1994 of the Reed Report on Services for Mentally Disordered Offenders there has been a welcome recognition that this is a priority area for development and the Commission is pleased to note an expansion of forensic psychiatric services. In May 1996, The Advisory Committee on Mentally Disordered Offenders, set up by the Government for a three year period to monitor and advise on action following the Reed recommendations, issued a Report (Department of Health/Home Office, 1996d) that noted the significant increase in medium secure beds. The target of 1,000 was already passed and 2,000 was thought achievable by the end of 1997. It was conceded, however, that progress was variable from place to place and that much remained to be done by way of local provision for both longer-term secure beds and low-level secure beds. The availability of forensic psychiatrists has not kept pace with this rapid expansion and some consultant posts are being filled by temporary locums. The High Security Psychiatric Services Commissioning Board now gives advice on co-ordinated commissioning of services at differing levels of security.

Commission experience confirms that, despite the expansion of some small units with forensic beds, in some areas demand greatly outstrips provision. Shortage of beds for behaviourally disturbed patients, as well as limited availability of appropriate community placements when they no longer need to be detained, has serious effects, including unacceptably long detention in police cells for patients waiting for admission. The impression gained from Commission Visits is echoed by observers outside the Commission (Murray, 1996). For example, Brown et al (1996), in an analysis of times spent by patients waiting for transfer to the Edenfield RSU, found the periods variable, with a minority of patients waiting 6 months or longer. The waiting times were significantly longer for those on transfers from prison, and particularly for patients from High Security Hospitals, in comparison with local referrals. There are problems also in finding secure places for patients transferred from prisons while on remand (Section 48). For example, at the Bentham Remand Ward at Ealing Hospital, staff have difficulty in passing on to appropriately secure units patients who are returned to the trial court with medical recommendations for a Hospital Order. Delays in implementing plans to expand secure provision are frustrating to those striving to provide service (*see also* 4.4.3)

West Berkshire Priority Care Services NHS Trust: Visit 20.2.97

Repeated postponements of plans for relocation and expansion of the Wallingford Clinic RSU service, the latest being attributed to the complexities of the Private Finance Initiative, are causing problems. Patients from the area who need a secure bed are being accommodated far away, while patients ready to move on have long waits for suitable placements.

Mentally disordered offenders present complex and challenging problems that call for attention from a range of agencies. When they are resistant to advice, or apt to move away without notice, the difficulties are compounded. Failures in communication between the different workers and agencies involved in such cases have been highlighted in several of the inquiries into homicides by mentally disordered people. Although serious violence to others by the mentally ill is rare, a substantial body of research (Monahan, 1996) shows that it is more likely to occur during an acute flare-up of psychosis, such as may follow a period of non-compliance with medication. The Commission welcomes the emphasis in the recommendations of the Advisory Committee on Mentally Disordered Offenders (Dept. of Health/Home Office, 1996d) on the importance of joint planning and delivery of services and stronger links between the departments of central government responsible for the co-ordination of services, including police, probation, courts, prisons, housing, social care and health. Guidance on inter-agency working, dealt with more generally in the publication *Building Bridges* (Dept. of Health, 1995c) is applied more specifically to mentally disordered offenders in a circular from the Home Office (1995) and accompanying good practice guide.

Implementation of the Crime (Sentences) Act 1997, which introduces mandatory sentences, could impact on services for mentally disordered offenders. The imposition of mandatory life sentences (save in exceptional circumstances) for persons guilty of a second 'serious' offence could mean that a number of mentally disordered offenders who are not found legally insane, and who might otherwise have been given Hospital Orders, will be committed to prison and will reach hospital, if at all, only via the uncertain and time-consuming prison transfer procedures. This could only add to the number of mentally disordered prisoners, which is already substantial, and increase the number of admissions to hospital of patients affected by exposure to the prison subculture.

The introduction of Hospital Directives for mentally disordered offenders, combining an initial committal to hospital with a sentence of imprisonment, means that a minimum period of detention can be imposed according to degree of culpability, a concept not hitherto applied to those deemed to be detainable on grounds of mental disorder. Initially, this will apply only to psychopaths, but Ministerial decision can extend it to other categories, as is already the case in Scotland and Northern Ireland.

The prospect of having more hospitalised mentally ill offenders under sentence of imprisonment, including life imprisonment, has alarmed some forensic psychiatrists (Eastman, 1997). They foresee doctors being reluctant to jeopardise the recovery of such patients by declaring them well enough to be diverted from continuity of care and exposed to a prison environment. Some of these patients would be likely to be retained in hospital longer than if they could be discharged directly to care in the community, thereby blocking beds, preventing the admission of other prospective patients and increasing the burden on the NHS.

10.8.2 Court Liaison Schemes

The continued development of schemes for the identification and assessment of mentally disordered offenders appearing before the criminal courts is to be welcomed, but in so far as they increase demand for hospital places for patients presenting management problems they are putting more pressure on beds already in short supply and indirectly encouraging premature discharges of non-forensic patients. However, the increase in numbers of patients, new to mental health services, is limited. The majority of referrals are of patients who have already had contact with psychiatric services. These schemes have reduced, but not abolished, the problem of mentally ill people being remanded to prisons. In spite of increased effort to identify and accommodate mentally disordered offenders, and in spite of the increase in transfers from prison to mental hospitals, recent research (Birmingham et al, 1996) shows a high prevalence of mental disorder, including acute psychosis, among prisoners on remand. Local schemes vary in scope and character, some employing a court-based community psychiatric nurse, others relying upon being called in by probation officers or court officials. Uncertainty about the future, when temporary Home Office funding ceases, can affect performance. The larger and better-established schemes (such as the Horseferry Road service in Westminster), employing a psychiatrist with access to beds in a Medium Secure Unit, result in a high proportion of referrals receiving Hospital Orders. Others, such as Salford and Wirral, employ a full-time Community Psychiatric Nurse. Some schemes 'divert' relatively few cases to community mental health services. This may be due to the nature of the clientele, but it may also reflect limited working relationships with probation and other community services. For instance, arrangements for the transport of patients from court to hospital sometimes causes difficulty. A Home Office circular (1995) emphasises the need, when dealing with mentally disordered offenders, for clearly defined participation at local level by all criminal justice, health and social service interests. A guidance document, *Probation and Health* (1996) points out that mentally disordered offenders may exhibit various combinations of mental illness, learning disability, substance abuse and sexual problems. Without effective collaboration between services, diversion into community care cannot work effectively

10.8.3 Section 41 Patients in Double Jeopardy?

Patients on Section 41 Restriction Orders are usually released from hospital conditionally, the conditions being set by a Tribunal or by the Home Office or both. Medical supervision and supervision by a Local Authority social worker or a probation officer are normally required, with reports made periodically to the Home Office. While living in the community on unexpired or undischarged Restriction Orders, patients are liable to recall to hospital by order of the Secretary of State.

On occasion, while still subject to Section 41 conditions, patients have been admitted to hospital on Section 2 or 3. Sometimes, this may have been considered a less restrictive intervention than recall and cancellation of their conditional discharge. However that may be, the issue arises whether it is lawful to apply this additional method of compulsory detention to a person already liable to be detained under Section 41. A case is currently before the Courts—*R v Managers of North West London Mental Health NHS Trust and the Secretary of State for the Home Department and another, ex parte S (The Times* 19 July 1996)—about the lawfulness of the application of Section 3 to a patient on conditional discharge from a Tribunal. The patient is appealing against the decision that Section 3 can be used in such circumstances.

10.9 Services for Adolescents

Although relatively few adolescents are detained under the Mental Health Act (see 3.1.5), the Commission is concerned to note, despite improvements and the increased participation of the independent sector, that provision remains uneven. Adolescents continue to be placed in adult facilities. This is unacceptable, although it is recognised that there may not be any other better options in particular cases. The Commission will continue to urge that adolescents are placed in an environment which is appropriate to age and stage of development.

Heron Lodge, Norfolk Mental Healthcare NHS Trust: Visit 21.7.95

It was found that a fifteen year old female had been admitted from a magistrates' court. This was said to be a rare, if not unique, event. The referring court was aware of the inappropriateness of the placement in an adult facility, but commended the high standard of care received by the patient in the circumstances.

Camlet Lodge Regional Secure Unit, Enfield Community Care NHS Trust: Visit 11.1.96

At the time of the visit a sixteen year old female was detained in the unit. The Trust were advised that the purchasers should be encouraged to collaborate to resolve deficiencies in the provision for both women and adolescents requiring treatment in conditions of medium security.

The Commission has had occasion to commend new developments in many areas.

Well Lane Young Persons' Centre, North Staffordshire Combined Healthcare NHS Trust: Visit 2.8.96

Commission members commended this 12 bedded unit for 11 to 17 year olds with a range of psychiatric problems. Particular attention was drawn to the dedicated education and social work support available and the consequential positive impression of a well run unit providing a high quality of service within attractive surroundings and making good use of the limited space available within an old building. The Commission has since been informed that, subject to securing Private Finance Initiative arrangements, a new hospital is planned which will include a unit for 10 children and adolescents.

Treatment facilities for adolescents in the North have increased and diversified.

Gardner Unit, Salford NHS Trust: Visit 1.3.96 and 5.9.96

This unit has established links with the McGuiness Unit and has focused its services on young people with mental illness, A high standard has been recorded in both educational and recreational facilities. However, activities were confined to the school day, resulting in absences from important lessons. Progress in a number of directions was noted at the later visit. Clinical psychology sessions had been introduced and the establishment in ASWs increased. Bedroom areas had improved and work was being undertaken on consent issues in relation to young people.

West Berkshire Priority Care NHS Trust: Visit 11.10.96

Commission members commented favourably on the 10-bedded adolescent unit as providing a pleasant environment with a good teaching facility.

It is hoped that increased facilities will prevent, in future, the need to include adolescent patients on an adult ward. Expansion of the facilities offered by the independent sector is considerable. Two wards catering for adolescents at St. Andrew's Hospital, Northampton, are to be supplemented in 1998 with the opening of a new learning disability unit on the school site. Educational provision in the independent sector is uneven. Accommodating adolescents away from local NHS facilities carries the drawback that many are placed far from home so that visits to patients are limited. Telephone communication becomes important, but incurs costs.

10.10 Mental Health Act—Some Areas of Difficulty

It is 14 years since the Mental Health Act came into force and the Commission remains of the view (expressed initially in the Fifth Biennial Report) that the Act should be subject to a full review.

In its monitoring of the Act, the Commission has come across increasing difficulties in the interpretation and application of some parts of it, as well as instances which illustrate possible serious deficiencies in its provisions, which have been referred to in previous Biennial Reports. Whilst any review of the Act and subsequent amendment is a matter for the Secretary of State and ultimately Parliament, it may be helpful to draw attention to three prominent areas of difficulty encountered by the Commission in the period under review.

10.10.1 Provision of Medical Recommendations

Ordinarily, only one doctor on the staff of an admitting hospital may provide a medical recommendation in support of an application for admission for assessment or treatment under the Act. With the introduction of NHS Trusts, recommendations are frequently and lawfully provided by doctors employed by the same Trust (but working at different hospitals) whilst, on occasion, recommendations are unlawfully provided by doctors employed by different Trusts, but on the staff of the same hospital, where the hospital is the responsibility of more than one Trust. This is primarily a difficulty of interpretation, but may also illustrate how some of the basic principles underlying the Act have been so overtaken by subsequent legal and service developments as to warrant review.

10.10.2 Definition of a Hospital and the Application of the Act

The procedures and safeguards set out in the Act are premised on a model of the hospital that was prevalent in the 1970s. The rapid diversification of types of facility in which mental health care under the Act is delivered, not only makes the Act at times difficult to apply correctly, but also calls into question the effectiveness of some of its safeguards. "Hospitals" for the purpose of the Mental Health Act come in increasingly different shapes and sizes. A recent query to the Commission illustrates some of the problems that arise. An in-patient service had moved from a conventional hospital to eight community homes (owned by the NHS Trust, and therefore a hospital for the purposes of the Mental Health Act) together with a separate assessment centre to which patients go during the day. The Commission was asked if it was possible to apply the provisions of the nurses holding powers (Section 5(4)) at the assessment centre, on the basis that it, together with the geographically separate community homes jointly constituted a hospital of which the patients were "in-patients": two legal prerequisites for the application of the nurses holding power.

10.10.3 The Nearest Relative

Two aspects of the provisions in the Act about the Nearest Relative continue to cause concern:

- The Commission continues to receive reports of instances where it is inappropriate for a person to remain as the Nearest Relative for the purposes of the Act: for instance where the patient has been abused, physically, emotionally or sexually by that person in the past. At present, there are no provisions in the Act for that person to be removed from exercising the functions of the Nearest Relative on these grounds.

- An application to a county court to appoint an acting Nearest Relative in respect of a patient detained under Section 2, has the effect of extending the patient's detention under that Section beyond 28 days and until the application is heard by the court. During that time, the patient has no right of application to a Mental Health Review Tribunal. The Commission has continued to be notified of a small number of instances where a patient's detention has been extended in this way. In one typical case the patient's detention was extended by a further 53 days. Whilst it may be possible to ameliorate such consequences by taking steps to enable court procedures to dispose of such applications speedily, the Commission would support an amendment to the Act whereby a right of application to a Tribunal accrued to the patient as soon as their detention was extended beyond 28 days in these circumstances.

REFERENCES

Age Concern (1992) *Other People's Money — Guidance on the responsibilities of formal carers in the NHS.*

Ashworth Hospital Authority (1996) *Care and Responsibility Training.* Liverpool: Centre for Aggression Management.

Banerjee, S., Bingley, W. and Murphy, E. (1995) *Deaths of Detained Patients: A Review of Reports of the Mental Health Act Commission.* London: Mental Health Foundation.

Barnes, M. (1996) Citizens in detention: The role of the Mental Health Act Commission in protecting the rights of detained patients. *Local Government Studies*, **22** (No. 3), 28–46.

Benefits Agency Medical Services (1995) *The Medical Adviser's Guide to Incapacity Benefits.* Leeds: Benefits Agency Publishing Services.

Birmingham, L., Mason, D. & Grubin, D. (1996) Prevalence of mental disorders in remand prisoners:consecutive case study. *British Medical Journal*, **313**, 1512–7.

Blom-Cooper, L. et al (1992) *Report of the Inquiry into Complaints about Ashworth Hospital.* Command 2028. London: H.M.S.O.

Blom-Cooper, L. et al (1995) *The Falling Shadow: One Patient's Mental Health Care.* London: Duckworth.

Blom-Cooper, L., Grounds, A., Guinan, P., Parker, A. & Taylor, M. (1996) *The Case of Jason Mitchell.* London: Duckworth.

Brown, P., McKenna, J.M. and Tomenson, B. (1996) Waiting for a bed in a regional secure unit. *Journal of Forensic Psychiatry*, **7**, 534–640.

Cantwell, R. & Harrison, G. (1996) Substance misuse in the severely mentally ill. *Advances in Psychiatric Treatment*, **2**, 117–124

Central Council for Education and Training in Social Work (1996) *Assuring Quality for Mental Health Social Work. Approval, Review and Inspection of Approved Social Worker (ASW) Programmes in England and Wales.* CCETSW.

Council of Europe (1996) *Report on the Visit to the United Kingdom carried out by the European Committee for the Prevention of Torture and Inhuman or Degrading Treatment or Punishment.* CPT/inf (96) 11. Council of Europe: Strasbourg.

Council of Europe (1996) *Final Response of the United Kingdom Government to the European Committee for the Prevention of Torture and Inhuman or Degrading Treatment.* CPT/inf 12. Council of Europe: Strasbourg.

Crawford, L, Devaux, M, Ferris R and Hayward, P (1997) *The Report into the Care and Treatment of Martin Mursell.* London: Camden and Islington Health Authority.

Creighton, J.H.M. (1995) Is it Time for a Formal Disciplinary Code for Psychiatric In-patients in England and Wales? *Medicine, Science and the Law*, 35, 65–68.

Department of Health (1994) *Guidance on the Discharge of Mentally Ill People and their Continuing Care in the Community.* HSG (94) 27.

Department of Health (1995) *In-Patients Formally Detained in Hospitals under the Mental Health Act 1983 and other Legislation: 1987–88 to 1992–93.* Statistical Bulletin 1995/4.

Department of Health: Local Authority Personal Social Services Statistics (1995) *Guardianship under the Mental Health Act 1983: England 1995.*

Department of Health (1995) *Building Bridges: A Guide to Arrangements for Inter-Agency Working for the Care and Protection of Severely Mentally Ill People.* London: Department of Health.

Department of Health (1996a) *In-Patients Formally Detained in Hospitals under the Mental Health Act 1983 and other Legislation: 1989–90 to 1994–95.* Statistical Bulletin 1996/10.

Department of Health (1996b) *Guidance on Supervised Discharge (after-care under supervision) and Related Provisions.* HSG (96) 11.

Department of Health (1996c) *Electoral Registration of Patients Detained under the Mental Health Act 1983.* HSG (96) 43.

Department of Health/Home Office (1996d) *Report of the Advisory Committee on Mentally Disordered Offenders.*

Department of Health (1996e) *The Spectrum of Care: Local Services for People with Mental Health Problems.*

Department of Health (1996f) *Approval of Doctors under Section 12 of the Mental Health Act 1983.* HSG (96) 3

Department of Health (1996g) *The Use of 'Trial Leave' under Section 17 of the Mental Health Act to Transfer Patients between Hospitals.* HSG (96) 28.

Department of Health (1997a) *In-Patients Formally Detained in Hospitals under the Mental Health Act 1983 and other Legislation: 1990–91 to 1995–96*. Statistical Bulletin 1997/4.

Department of Health (1997b) *The Patients' Charter: Mental Health Services.* London: Department of Health.

Eastman, N. (1997) Hybrid justice: proposals for the mentally disordered in the Crime [sentences] Bill. *Psychiatric Bulletin*, **21**, 129–131.

Fennell, P. (1996) *Treatment without Consent: Law, Psychiatry and the Treatment of Mentally Disordered People since 1845*. London: Routledge.

Frost, C. (1996) *The Impact of Illicit Substance Use within Mental Health Services.* Liverpool: Aintree Hospitals NHS Trust.

Holmes, G. (1996) Bringing about change in a psychiatric hospital: The Patients' Council at Shelton two years on. *Clinical Psychology Forum. 95*

Home Office (1995) *Mentally Disordered Offenders Inter-Agency Working.* Circular 12/95.

Jones, R. (1996) *Mental Health Act Manual.* (5th ed) London: Sweet and Maxwell.

Johnson, S. et al (1997) *London's Mental Health. Report to the King's Fund London Commission.* London: King's Fund.

Law Commission (1995) *Mental Incapacity.* Paper 231, London: H.M.S.O.

Liebling, H. & McKeown, M. (1995) Staff perceptions of illicit drug use within a special hospital. In British Psychological Society. *Criminal Behaviour, Perceptions, Attributions and Rationality. Issues in Criminological and Legal Psychology* No 19

London Ambulance Service (1996) *Admitting Mentally Ill Patients to Hospital.*

Mental Health Act Commission and the Sainsbury Centre (1997) *The National Visit. A one-day visit to 309 acute psychiatric wards by The Mental Health Act Commission in collaboration with The Sainsbury Centre for Mental Health.* The Sainsbury Centre for Mental Health.

Morrison, P. and Lehane,M. (1996) A study of official seclusion records. *International Journal of Nursing Care*, **33**, (No.2) 223–235.

Murphy, E. (1996) The past and future of special hospitals. *Journal of Mental Health*, 5, 475–482.

Murray, K. (1996) The use of beds in NHS Medium Secure Units in England. *Journal of Forensic Psychiatry*, 7, 504–524.

NHS Executive (1994) *Collection of ethnic group data for admitted patients.* EL (94)77.

Probation and Health (1996) *A Guidance Document Aimed at Promoting Effective Working between the Health and Probation Services.* London: H.M.S.O.

Revolving Doors Agency (1995) *The Use of Section 136 Mental Health Act in Three Inner London Police Divisions.* Report to the Home Office. London.

Richardson, G. (1995) Openness, order and regulation in a therapeutic setting. In J.H.M.Creighton (Ed.) *Psychiatric Patient Violence. Risk and Response.* London: Duckworth.

Ritchie, J.H. (1994) *Report of the Inquiry into the Care and Treatment of Christopher Clunis.* London: H.M.S.O.

Royal College of Psychiatrists (1993) *Consensus Report on the Use of High Dosage Antipsychotic Medication.* Council Report CR 26. London: Royal College of Psychiatrists.

Royal College of Psychiatrists (1995) *Strategies for the Management of Disturbed and Violent Patients in Psychiatric Hospitals.* Council Report 41. London: Royal College of Psychiatrists.

Royal College of Psychiatrists (1995) The *ECT Handbook; The Second Report of the Special Committee on ECT.* (Council Report 39) London: Royal College of Psychiatrists.

Royal College of Psychiatrists (1996) *Confidential Enquiry into Homicides and Suicides by Mentally Ill People.* London: Royal College of Psychiatrists.

Sackett, K. (1996) Discharges from Section 3 of the Mental Health Act 1983; changes in practice. *Health Trends,* **28** (No.2), 64–66.

Shepherd, G., Murray, A. & Muijen, M. (1994) *Relative Values.* London: The Sainsbury Centre for Mental Health.

Smith, J. & Hucker, S. (1994) Schizophrenia and substance abuse. *British Journal of Psychiatry,* **165**, 13–21.

Thomas, B. (1995) Caught in the front line. *Nursing Times,* **91**, (No. 45) 39–9.

Thompson, C . (1994) The use of high dose anti-psychotic medication. *British Journal of Psychiatry,* **164**, 448–458.

Welsh Office (1997) *Use of the Mental Health Act 1983 (and Other Legislation) in NHS Hospitals in Wales.* SDB 9/97. Government Statistical Service.

Working Group (1996) *Report [to the Department of Health] on Managers' Review of Detention.* July 1996

Zarb, G. (Ed.) (1996) *Social Security and Mental Health. Report of the SSAC Workshop.* London: H.M.S.O.

Zigmond, A. (1995) Special Care wards: are they special. *Psychiatric Bulletin*, **19**, 310-312.

Zito Trust (1996) *Learning the Lessons.* 2nd Ed. London: Zito Trust.

APPENDIX 1

MENTAL HEALTH ACT COMMISSION MEMBERS 1995-97

CHAIRMAN: Viscountess Ruth Runciman OBE
VICE CHAIRMAN: Until 31/12/96   Nigel Pleming QC
                 From 01/04/97   Dr Richard Williams

LAY Members

Mrs A Anderson	Mrs E Owen	Mrs J Spencer
Dr T Blowers	Ms J Rogers	Mrs B Stroll
Mrs M E Coleman	Mrs S Spence	Mr M Taylor

LAY Visiting Members

Miss C Allison	Ms F Eliot	Ms M Nettle
Ms C Bamber	Mrs J Gossage	Miss I Reinbach
Mr B Burke	Mr S Hedges	Mr S Weldon
Ms H Burke	Ms J Hesmondhalgh	Mr M Wilce
Mrs A Cooney	Mr G Kerr	Mr E Wong

LEGAL Members

Mrs C Bond	Professor M Gunn	Mrs J Olsen
Mrs S Breach	Mr J Horne	Mr A Parkin
Professor B Dimond	Professor M Jones	Mrs J Patterson
Mr A Eldergill	Mrs M Lloyd	Mr R Robinson
Ms C Grimshaw	Ms G McMorrow	Ms L Sinclair

LEGAL Visiting Members

Mr H Chapman	Mr D Hewitt	Ms C Parker
Mr P Croughton	Ms D R Johnson	Mr A Robinson
Ms G Downham	Mr G Jones	Mr J Sedgman
Mr M Frost	Ms A Lawrence	Ms J Tweedie
Mr J Halliwell	Ms A Lee	Mr T Wrigglesworth
Miss A Henry	Miss L Marriott	

MEDICAL Members

Dr D Black	Dr M Harper	Dr E Parker
Dr O Daniels	Dr P Hettiaratchy	Dr R Philpott
Dr C Davies	Dr J Holliday	Dr G Pryce
Dr D Dunleavy	Dr V Jain	Dr B Sekhawat
Dr S Fernando	Dr T Jerram	Dr S Soni
Dr S Francis	Dr G Mathur	Dr M Swan
Dr N Gittleson	Dr E Mendelson	Dr T Zigmond

MEDICAL Visiting Members

Dr C Berry	Dr H Edwards	Dr C Foster
Dr I Mian		

NURSING Members

Mr R Bevan	Mr M Hill	Mr A Morley
Mr E Chitty	Mrs S Lee	Mr A Persaud
Mr A Cooper	Mr N Lees	Mrs C Selim
Mr R Earle	Mr C McCarthy	Mr R Wix
Mr H Field	Mr D McCarthy	
Mr M Graham	Mr H McClarron	

NURSING Visiting Members

Mrs E Abrahams	Mr L Dodds	Ms S McKeever
Mr C Aggett	Mrs M DosAnjos	Ms P McKenzie
Mrs C Baptiste-Cyrus	Mr S Gannon	Mr M Naylor
Mrs K Berry	Mr D Hill	Ms E O'Farrell
Ms M Caswell	Mr N Khan	Mr S Pierre
Mr H Davis	Mr J Marlow	Mrs R Riddle
Mr A Deery	Miss M McCann	Mr S Stratton

PSYCHOLOGY Members

Dr J Barrie Ashcroft	Mr J Sharich	Mr L Wilson
Mr A Dabbs	Ms P Spinks	Professor A Yates
Ms E Rassaby	Mr D Torpy	

SOCIAL WORKER Members

Mr A Ball	Ms M Halstead	Mr B Morgan
Ms L Bolter	Mr G Halliday	Miss I Nutting
Mr R Brown	Ms L Jones	Mr E Prtak
Mr J Cohen	Mr R Lingham	Mr A Williamson
Mr T S Evans	Mrs V Lipscomb	
Ms E Frost	Mrs C Llewelyn-Jones	

SOCIAL WORKER Visiting Members

Mr R Bamlett	Mr P Howes	Mrs H Ross
Mr M Beebe	Mr S Klein	Ms Y Saloojee
Mr J Cooley	Mrs A Kelbrick	Mrs C Sheehy
Mr A Drew	Mr D Lee	Ms A Shields
Mrs J Endean	Ms H Lewis	Mrs H Thomas
Mrs J Freeman	Mrs J Lewis	Mr J Walker
Mr M Golightley	Mrs M Madden	Ms C Whiting
Mrs J Healy	Mrs P McCaig	Mrs R Williams-Flew
Ms G Heath	Mrs S McMillan	Mr B Windle
Mr M Hefferman	Mr J Moran	Mr A Wright
Ms P Heslop	Mr R Nichol	
Mrs C Hewitt	Ms M Napier	
Ms B Howard	Mr R Plumb	

SPECIALIST Members

Mr C Curran	Mr A Milligan	Dr R Ryall
Ms L Ingham	Inspector N North	Mr N Weaver
Mr G Lakes	Ms J Prior	Professor D West
Mrs L Mason	Ms M Purcell	

SPECIALIST Visiting Members

Ms B Allwood	Mr Y Marsen-Luther	Ms D Steele
Ms N Chesworth-Wigger	Mr R Mason	Mr M Wiseman
Mr R Fletcher	Mrs L Meade	Mr T Wishart
Miss M Garner	Mrs J Meredith	Mr J Woolmore
Ms G Gower	Mrs A Navarro	Mr T Wright
Ms P Letts	Mr K Patel	
Canon F Longbottom	Ms M Southwell	

APPENDIX 2

SECTIONS 58 and 57 APPOINTEES

Section 58 Appointed Doctors

July 1995 — March 1997

Dr R T Abed
Dr P Abraham
Dr M D Alldrick
Dr D Battin
Dr S Baxter
Dr S M Benbow
Dr C Berry
Dr K Bergman
Dr M S Bethell
Dr D J Bevington
Dr K G M Bhakta
Dr E Birchall
Dr A Black
Dr R N Bloor
Dr A J Blowers
Dr R S Bluglass
Dr J Bolton
Dr N Bouras
Dr C E Boyd
Dr C Brook
Dr A C Brown
Dr M Browne
Dr A W Burke
Dr D C Calvert
Dr M D Cashman
Dr R Chitty
Dr A Clarkson
Dr M P Cleary
Dr J Cockburn
Dr M Conway
Dr S Craske

Dr J Cuthill
Dr I Davidson
Dr C Davies
Dr J Davies
Dr M H Davies
Dr N Davies
Dr J Davis
Dr K Davison
Dr K A Day
Dr J C Denmark
Dr N D M Desai
Dr M Devakumar
Dr R Devine
Dr D Dick
Dr G O Duborg
Dr D L F Dunleavy
Dr J Dunlop
Dr H Eaton
Dr H Edwards
Dr S Edwards
Dr V M Evans
Dr A F Fairbarn
Dr G S Feggetter
Dr T W Fenton
Dr S Fernando
Dr J Fisher
Dr M Forth
Dr A F Francis
Dr R G Gall
Dr E G Gallagher
Dr C Ghosh

Dr N L Gittleson
Dr M D A P
Goonatilleke
Dr E B Gordon
Dr C Green
Dr E M Gregg
Dr J S Grimshaw
Dr J Hailstone
Dr M A Harper
Dr B G Harwin
Dr A Hauck
Dr B E Heine
Dr M Hession
Dr P Hettiaratchy
Dr S Hettiaratchy
Dr O Hill
Dr L Homewood
Dr R J S Hughes
Dr R K G Hughes
Dr J A Hutchinson
Dr M Humphreys
Dr G S Ibrahimi
Dr H D James
Dr S R N James
Dr P M Jefferys
Dr J Jenkins
Dr B John
Dr D V Jones
Dr F A Judelson
Dr A C Kaeser
Dr G Kanakaratnam

Dr A M P Kellam
Dr J Kellett
Dr H Kelly
Dr T A Kerr
Dr K Khan
Dr D Kohen
Dr L M Kremer
Dr G E Langley
Dr M Launer
Dr A R M Lewis
Dr L I Liebling
Dr B A Lowe
Dr J S Lyon
Dr S Malik
Dr G N Mathur
Dr M Matthews
Dr D McVitie
Dr L G Measey
Dr G Mehta
Dr I H Mian
Dr G Milner
Dr A Minto
Dr N Minton
Dr B Moore
Dr J D Mumford
Dr H Myers
Dr G Nanayakkara
Dr T E Nelson
Dr H Nissenbaum
Dr J G Noble
Dr M O'Brien

Dr S Olivieri

Dr R F Orr

Dr S S Palia

Dr A G Patel

Dr J E Phillips

Dr R M Philpott

Dr I G Pryce

Dr T Rajamanickam

Dr S C Rastogi

Dr B Rathod

Dr N J Renton

Dr M Rice

Dr E H Richards

Dr J Roberts

Dr J Robertson

Dr A J Rugg

Dr P Saleem

Dr M A Salih

Dr M S Samuel

Dr G A Sampson

Dr P N Sarkar

Dr N P Sebaratnum

Dr M Segal

Dr A Silverman

Dr M J Smith

Dr S Soni

Dr V Spotswood

Dr D A Stephens

Dr M Swan

Dr R L Symonds

Dr L Tarlo

Dr R Thavasothy

Dr R Thaya-Paran

Dr I G Thomson

Dr R M Toms

Dr N W F Tyre

Dr P Urwin

Dr H M Verma

Dr G D P Wallen

Dr A M Walsh

Dr D J Ward

Dr P E Watson

Dr K Weeks

Dr Y V Wiley

Dr A M Wilson

Dr G C Wijeyeratne

Dr S Wood

Dr E Wright

Dr R Yurarajan

Dr A S Zigmond

Section 57 Panel Members

Lay Members

Dr A Blowers

Mrs J Hanham

Mrs R Lewis

Mrs M Morris

Ms M Nettle

Mr G Smith

Legal Members

Mrs C Bennett

Professor B Dimond

Mr M Edwardes-Evans

Ms C Parker

Mr A Parkin

Medical Members

Dr E Carr

Dr C Davies

Dr K Day

Dr D Dunleavy

Dr E Gordon

Dr J Grimshaw

Dr M Harper

Dr P Jefferys

Dr G E Langley

Dr F Oyebode

Dr L Tarlo

Nursing Members

Mr E Chitty

Mr H Davis

Mrs R Fraser

Mrs A Land

Ms G Linton

Mr C McCarthy

Mr T Peel

Mr H Teaney

Pharmacy Members

Mr A Milligan

Psychology Members

Mr J Pinschof

Mr D Torpy

Mr L Wilson

Social Workers

Mr A Ball

Rev B Lillington

Mr R Lingham

Specialist

Archdeacon A Hawes

Mr G Lakes

Dr R Ryall

APPENDIX 3

SUMMARY OF FINANCES

STATEMENT OF CHIEF EXECUTIVE'S RESPONSIBILITIES IN RESPECT OF THE ACCOUNTS

The Chief Executive is required under the National Health Services Act 1977 to prepare accounts for each financial year. The Secretary of State, with the approval of the Treasury, directs that these accounts present fairly the receipts and payments of the authority for that period. In preparing those accounts, the Chief Executive is required to:

- Apply on a consistent basis accounting policies laid down by the Secretary of State with the approval of the Treasury.

- Make judgements and estimates which are reasonable and prudent.

- State whether applicable accounting standards have been followed, subject to any material departures disclosed and explained in the account.

The Chief Executive confirms that they have complied with the above requirements in preparing the accounts.

The Chief Executive is responsible for keeping proper accounting records which disclose with reasonable accuracy at any time the financial position of the authority and to enable them to ensure that the accounts comply with requirements outlined in the above mentioned direction by the Secretary of State. They are also responsible for safeguarding the assets of the authority and hence for taking reasonable steps for the prevention and detection of fraud and other irregularities.

By Order of the Board

Signed : Chairman .... Dated: 18.9. 1996

Chief Executive ...William Bingley... Dated: 18.9. 1996

STATEMENT OF FINANCE DIRECTOR'S RESPONSIBILITIES

As Director of Finance I am responsible for:

- The maintenance of financial records appropriate to the activities of the authority.

- The establishment and monitoring of a system of internal control.

- The establishment of arrangements for the prevention of fraud and corruption.

- The preparation of annual financial statements which present fairly the financial position of the authority and the results of its operations.

In fulfilment of these responsibilities I confirm the financial statements set out on pages 3 to 7 attached, have been compiled from and are in accordance with the financial records maintained by the authority and with the accounting standards and policies for the NHS approved by the Secretary of State.

Signed :   Finance Director *Roberson*.... Dated: 18/9 1996

AUDITOR'S REPORTS ON THE HEALTH AUTHORITY ACCOUNTS

We certify that we have completed the audit of the financial statement on pages 3 to 7 attached, which have been prepared in accordance with the accounting policies relevant to the National Health Service.

RESPECTIVE RESPONSIBILITIES OF DIRECTORS AND AUDITORS

As described above, the Chief Executive is responsible for the preparation of financial statements. It is our responsibility to form an independent opinion, based on our audit on those statements, and to report our opinion to you.

BASIS OF OPINION

We carried out our audit in accordance with part 1 of the National Health Service and Community Care Act 1990 and the Code of Practice issued by the Audit Commission, which requires compliance with relevant auditing standards.

Our audit included examination, on a test basis, of evidence relevant to the amounts and disclosures in the financial statements. It also included an assessment of the significant estimates and judgements made by the authority in the preparation of the financial statements, and of whether the accounting policies are appropriate to the authority's circumstances, consistently applied and adequately disclosed.

We planned and performed our audit so as to obtain all the information and explanations which we considered necessary in order to provide us with sufficient evidence to give reasonable assurance that the financial statements are free from material misstatement, whether caused by fraud or other irregularity or error. In forming our opinion we also evaluated the overall adequacy of the presentation of information in the financial statements.

OPINION

In our opinion the financial statements present fairly the receipts and payments of the Mental Health Act Commission for the year ended 31 March 1996

Signed :   Auditor .... Dated:..**27.9.**..1996

MENTAL HEALTH ACT COMMISSION SPECIAL HEALTH AUTHORITY

RECEIPTS AND PAYMENTS ACCOUNTS FOR THE PERIOD

1 APRIL 1995 – 31 MARCH 1996

RECEIPTS	Notes	1995-1996	1994-1995
Cash Advances from DH	3	£2,706,993.00	£2,650,886.00
Other receipts		£3,436.00	£13,297.00
Patient Information Leaflet Sponsorship		Nil	£3,141.00
		£2,710,429.00	£2,667,324.00

PAYMENTS

Surplus (Deficit) from operations		£1,476.00	£11,937.00
Other Receipts/Payments		Nil	Nil
Appropriations		Nil	Nil
EXCESS OF RECEIPTS OVER PAYMENTS (PAYMENTS OVER RECEIPTS)			
		£1,476.00	£11,937.00

MENTAL HEALTH ACT COMMISSION SPECIAL HEALTH AUTHORITY

STATEMENT OF BALANCES AS AT 31 MARCH 1996

	Notes	1995-1996	1994-1995
Balance at beginning of year		£8,316.00	£14,418.00
Return of 1993/94 receipts		N/A	-£4,742.00
Excess Receipts over payment		£1,476.00	£11,937.00
Amount returned to Department		-£1,476.00	-£11,937.00
Difference between cash held at 31 March 1994 and 1995		-£1,960.00	-£1,360.00
Balance at 31 March 1995	6	£6,356.00	£8,316.00

The notes on Pages 5, 6 & 7 form part of these accounts.

MENTAL HEALTH ACT COMMISSION SPECIAL HEALTH AUTHORITY

NOTES TO THE ACCOUNTS

1) a) These accounts are drawn up in a form directed by the Secretary of State and approved by the Treasury.

   b) The tax element for 1995/96 has not been paid during the 1995/96 financial year and has therefore not been taken into account.

2) a) For 1995/1996 actual figures were extracted from the accounting records of the Department of Health for all items disclosed in Notes 3, 4 and 5, with the exception of Notes 5c, d, g and 6c, all of which have been taken from local records.

   b) In 1995/96, as in previous years, the notification of payments made by the Department of Health on behalf of the MHAC could not be reconciled with the MHAC's records. There was a net imbalance of £109,359, which is represented by more additional payments in the records of the Department of Health than authorised by the MHAC. The Department of Health investigated the difference and concluded that it was probably a result of mis-codings, made centrally by the Department of Health, of payments between the MHAC and the Mental Health Review Tribunal. The consequence of having to accept these erroneous figures is that the MHAC is recording an overspend of £72,078 against its cash limit, rather than an actual underspend of £37,281 — See Annex A for details.

Note *All balance of funds at the end of each financial year are retained by the Department of Health. Receipts are now shown as being received and returned in the same financial year.*

3) RECEIPTS

	1995-1996	1994-1995
a — Advances from Vote 1 Subhead E32A, E32B and E32C	£1,808,168.00	£1,953,481.00
b — Advances from Vote1 Subhead E32D	£843,715.00	£698,705.00
c — Advances from Welsh Office	£57,000.00	Nil
d — Advances from (Refunds to) Vote 1 E32A & E32B Suspense Account	-£1,890.00	-£1,300.00
Other receipts	£3,436.00	£13,297.00
Patient Information Leaflet Sponsorship	Nil	£3,141.00
	£2,710,429.00	£2,667,324.00

4) SALARIES

	1995-1996	1994-1995
a — Staff Salaries	£391,445.00	£426,799.00
b —National Insurance Contribution		
— Employer	£28,221.00	£30,751.00
c — Superannuation	£51,343.00	£53,766.00
d — Agency Costs	£2,670.00	£4,052.00
	£473,679.00	£515,368.00

5) OTHER OPERATING PAYMENTS

	1995-1996	1994-1995
a — Accommodation	£103,875.00	£64,793.00
b — Stationery, telephone, postage, common services, travel & subsistence etc.	£223,755.00	£107,125.00
c — Payments for purchase, construction or adaptation of premises	£2,643.00	£1,888.00
d — Plant and equipment	£39,833.00	£9,591.00
e — Members' Fees and Expenses	£866,603.00	£1,179,894.00
f — Second Opinion doctors' Fees and Expenses	£755,145.00	£660,179.00
g — Miscellaneous Expenditure	£225,757.00	£88,022.00
h — SOAD Training	£17,663.00	£25,386.00
i — Patient Information Leaflet	Nil	£3,141.00
	£2,235,274.00	£2,140,019.00

6) CASH BALANCE AT 31 MARCH

	1995-1996	1994-1995
a — Cash held by Members	£6,293.00	£8,183.00
b — Cash at Bank	Nil	Nil
c — Cash in hand (Petty cash)	£63.00	£133.00
	£6,356.00	£8,316.00

7) CASH LIMITS

The accounts of health authorities are subject to cash limit controls. A Cash limit is a predetermined limit on the spending (in cash terms) of health authorities. Each health authority is required to contain its net revenue outgoings or net capital payments in the year within the approved cash limit. In the particular case of the Mental Health Act Commission Special Health Authority, all expenditure has been subject to notified cash limits with the exception of the accommodation charges, which remains funded centrally by the Department of Health, and the Patient Information Leaflet Sponsorship Fund which does not form part of the cash limit.

A statement of net over/underspending of this Authority against the approved cash limit for the year ended 31 March is set out below:

		REVENUE
	1995–1996	1994–1995
Cash Limit	£2,533,000.00	£2,617,000.00
Charge against Cash Limit	£2,605,078.00	2,587,453.00
Underspending	N/A	£29,547.00
Overspending	£72,078.00	N/A

THE MENTAL HEALTH ACT COMMISSION

ACCOUNTS DIRECTION

Secretary of State, with the approval of the Treasury, in pursuance of Section of the National Health Service Act 1977 hereby gives the following direction:

In this direction, unless the context otherwise requires —

"the Act" means the National Health Service Act 1977;

"the authority" means the Mental Health Act Commission.

The statement of accounts which it is the duty of the authority to prepare in respect of the financial year ended 31 March 1996 shall be as set out in the following paragraphs and Schedule.

The statement of accounts of the authority shall comprise:

    a. a foreword;
    b. a receipts and payments account;
    c. a statement of cash and bank balances;
    d. such notes as may be necessary for the purposes referred to in paragraph 4 below.

The statement of accounts shall properly present the receipts and payments for the year and the cash and bank balances as at the end of the financial year. Subject to the foregoing requirement, the statement of accounts shall also, without limiting the information given and as described in the Schedule, meet:

    a. the accounting and disclosure requirements of the Companies Act. The disclosure exemptions permitted by the Companies Act will not apply unless specifically authorised by the Secretary of State with the approval of Treasury;

    b. best commercial accounting practice including accounting standards issued or adopted by the Accounting Standards Boards;

    c. all relevant guidance given in *"Government Accounting"* and in *"Trading Accounts: A Guide for Government Departments and Non-Departmental Public Bodies"* and in the *"NHS Manual for Accounts"*;

    d. any disclosure and accouting requrements which the Secretary of State or Treasury may issue from time to time;

Insofar as these are appropriate to the authority and are in force for the financial period for which the statement of accounts is to be prepared.

Dated...**6 September**...1995

Signed by the authority of the Secretary of State for Health

Signed ...*J C Dobson*...

Assistant Secretary
NHS Executive HQ
Department of Health

Annex A

MENTAL HEALTH ACT COMMISSION SPECIAL HEALTH AUTHORITY — LOCAL RECORDS

RECEIPTS AND PAYMENTS ACCOUNTS FOR THE PERIOD 1 APRIL 1995–31 MARCH 1996

RECEIPTS

	Notes	1995–1996
Cash Advances from DH	3	£2,597,634.00
Other receipts		£3,436.00
Patient Information Leaflet Sponsorship		Nil
		£2,601,070.00

PAYMENTS

	Notes	1995–1996
Salaries	4	£550,284.00
Patient Information Leaflet Sponsorship	5	£2,049,310.00
		£2,599,594.00
Surplus from operations		£1,476.00
Other Receipts/Payments		Nil
Appropriations		Nil
		£1,476.00

ACCOUNTS USING MENTAL HEALTH ACT
COMMISSION LOCAL RECORDS

3) RECEIPTS	1995–1996
a — Advances from Vote 1 Subhead E32A, E32B and E32C	£1,693,528.00
b — Advances from Vote 1 Subhead E32D	£848,996.00
c — Advances from Welsh Office	£57,000.00
d — Advances from (Refunds to) Vote 1 E32A & E32B Suspense Account	-£1,890.00
Other receipts	£3,436.00
Patient Information Leaflet Sponsorship	Nil
	£2,601,070.00

4) SALARIES	1995–1996
Total Staff Salaries including Agency Costs	£550,284.00

5) OTHER OPERATING PAYMENTS	1995–1996
a — Accommodation	£103,875.00
b — Stationery, telephone, postage, common services, travel & subsistence etc.	£152,431.00
c — Payments for purchase, construction or adaptation of premises	£2,643.00
d — Plant and equipment	£39,833.00
e — Members' Fees and Expenses	£858,669.00
f — Second Opinion doctors' Fees and Expenses	£646,036.00
g — Miscellaneous Expenditure	£225,757.00
h — SOAD Training	£20,066.00
i — Patient Information Leaflet	Nil
	£2,049,310.00

MENTAL HEALTH ACT COMMISSION SPECIAL HEALTH AUTHORITY

STATEMENT OF BALANCES AS AT 31 MARCH 1996

	Notes	1995–1996
Balance at beginning of year		£8,316.00
Excess Receipts over payment		£1,476.00
Amount returned to Department		-£1,476.00
Difference between cash held at 31 March 1994 and 1995		-£1,960.00
	6	£6,356.00

6) CASH BALANCE AT 31 MARCH		1995–1996
a — Cash held by Members		£6,293.00
b — Cash at Bank		£0.00
c — Cash in hand (Petty cash)		£63.00
		£6,356.00

7) CASH LIMITS	1995–1996
Cash Limit	£2,533,000.00
Charge against Cash Limit	£2,495,719.00
Underspending	£37,281.000
Overspending	N/A

APPENDIX 4

MENTAL HEALTH ACT COMMISSION PUBLICATIONS

Guidance Notes (formerly called Practice Notes)

Practice Note 1 — June 1993
"Guidance on the administration of Clozapine and other treatments requiring blood tests under the provision of Part IV of the Mental Health Act 1983"

Practice Note 2 — March 1994
"Nurses; the administration of medicines for mental disorder and the Mental Health Act"

Practice Note 3 — March 1994
"Section 5(2) of the 1983 Mental Health Act and transfers"

Practice Note 4 — May 1996
"Section 17 and 18 of the Mental Health Act 1983"

Practice Note 5 — July 1996
"Guidance on issues relating to the administration of the Mental Health Act in nursing homes registered to receive detained patients"

Guidance Note 1 — December 1996
"Guidance to Health Authorities: The Mental Health Act 1983"

Guidance Note 2 — December 1996
"GP's and the Mental Health Act"

Guidance Note 3 — July 1997
"Guidance on the treatment of Anorexia Nervosa under the Mental Health Act 1983"

Position Paper

Position Paper 1 — January 1997
"Research involving detained patients"

APPENDIX 5

EQUAL OPPORTUNITIES

POLICY STATEMENT

The Mental Health Act Commission is committed to the eradication of discrimination and the promotion of Equal Opportunities in all its services. The Commission will therefore discharge all its duties recognising that every individual has a legal and moral right to an equal and non-discriminatory high quality service.

All staff, Commission members and appointees therefore will:

- provide an equal service to all regardless of their age, colour, culture, gender, health, status, mental ability, mental health, offending background, physical ability, political beliefs, race, religion, sexuality or other specific factors which result in discrimination;

- in the exercise of their duties be committed to the promotion of good practice and equal access to all service users by purchasers and providers of mental health services taking into account our diverse society.

The Mental Health Act Commission will take action through the quality assurance and monitoring process to ensure the implementation of its policies which are above.

In turn all staff, Commission members and appointees will expect that all those who receive a service from the Commission will not use offensive language or actions, harass or victimise or act in a manner that is discriminatory and oppressive.

IMPLEMENTATION

Three Key areas:

- **Monitoring and Quality Assurance;**
- **Training and Development;**
- **Service Provision.**

Five Goals:

- To be committed to the identification of unequal and discriminatory services in the mental health field;
- To establish an effective monitoring and quality assurance system;
- To set specific foci for Commission activities - eg: women's issues and race and culture;
- To build in Equal Opportunities awareness into the development of members and staff;
- To increase the number of under-represented groups amongst staff, Commission members and appointees.

These measures aim to enhance public understanding of the Mental Health Act Commission's commitment to Equal Opportunities.

INDEX